Excelsior:
Upward & Onward
The Power of Self-Affirmation

By

Dr. Johnny Mac Allen

PublishAmerica
Baltimore

First printing

ISBN: 1-4137-3149-X
PUBLISHED BY PUBLISHAMERICA, LLLP
www.publishamerica.com
Baltimore

Printed in the United States of America

DEDICATION

To Lana. Your counsel, dedication, and tender spirit has been and continues to be an inspiration.

ACKNOWLEDGMENTS

*To Jedidiah Abrams for his
technical contributions and his
dedication to the finished manuscript.*

*Also, to all those who have in some way
contributed to the completion of the
book through their suggestions,
recommendations, and support.*

*I would also like to thank
PublishAmerica's Briana Finui
for her dedication, patience, and
commitment in the editing process.*

TABLE OF CONTENTS

Overview

Here is a starting point for you, the one desiring to improve your present existence and to help you on your way to "self-improvement."

This is a book for all people, the young just starting out in life, the professional reaching a critical career decision, and even the one who has simply ceased to believe in himself.

This book is designed to enhance your self-confidence and to assist you in constructing a solid and self-supporting foundation, built with proven principles, all of which are cited by example and instruction. You will redefine your personal goals, or perhaps set them for the first time.

The underlying theme of this text is to instill self-confidence and to develop in you a philosophy of a life of contribution by investing in yourself.

This will be a catalyst to help you reach your full potential and to fulfill God's purpose for your life by believing in yourself. You will find affirmation statements to be used as constant reminders of your personal worth. A literature list contains recommended readings by authorities in the area of self-improvement.

In short, the message to you is: "Yes, I can!"

My personal code of self-respect

I am valuable because God created me with an inner value and worth. I do not have to earn it.

I nurture self-respect as I understand and internalize my basic inner value. The value is there. I do not have to achieve it. I already have it. My challenge is to nurture and protect it from getting jaded or twisted by the values of a success-at-any-cost oriented society.

If I can avoid the trap of trying to possess success or adorn myself with success at the expense of others, I can easily live with self-respect. It will be more important to me to do things to protect my value—the marvelous gift I've been given—to other people. That is the primary motivation for being the best I can be.

My worth is my word. I make commitments, and I do what I say I will do. This is more than just important to me—it is crucial.

I say to others: "I am valuable, as you are valuable. We will make a value exchange. I will offer you the best I have, and I assume you will give me your best in return."

Preface

According to researchers, American corporations reinvent themselves every three-to-five years, and information on the Internet doubles every 2.8 years. Knowledge, say the experts, is doubling every five years, so where does that place you in the spectrum? In other words, have you "reinvented" yourself recently? As Robert H. Schuller stated in his 1997 book, *If It's Going to Be It's up to Me.* Yes, it is up to you because life only gets better when YOU get better. You want a helping hand? It's at the end of your wrist. A Chinese proverb asks, when's the best time to plant a tree? Answer: 20 years ago. When is the second best time? TODAY! And today you can begin to make that investment in yourself.

The problem is that we as a country don't read very much and even when we do, it's usually material that will serve for a brief period of time only, never to be transferred from short-term to long-term memory. There once was a gap between those who had wealth and material and those who did not. Today, the discrepancy is between those who have knowledge and those who don't have knowledge. Sir Hugh Rigby, the great English surgeon was once asked, "What makes a great surgeon?" He replied that he didn't think it was manual dexterity. No he said, "Some just know more than others." Some take it upon themselves to rebuild their confidence regardless of the circumstances and life's challenges. Instead, they make it their goal in life to be more informed, and better read than anyone around them. And more times than not, this results in better leadership abilities, promotions, and sought after opinions by those who respect their knowledge and expertise. And interestingly enough, it has nothing to do with a formal education.

According to various research studies, America's college students are not avid readers. And regretfully, only a small student minority understands the need to absorb information outside of the classroom. Compound this with the fact that only five percent of the population will either buy or read a book this year, and one can see the advantage of a self-educated improvement program.

Remember, there is nothing you can do that a book will not help you do better and if you can read and don't, you're no better off than someone who can't read at all.

This book however, is NOT a definitive work on anything. It is designed to introduce you to concepts and principles that have helped me over the years as well as my students, and to point you in the direction of self-affirmation and self-improvement. It will also provide you an opportunity as the great educator Robert Maynard Hutchins would say, to join in "The Great Conversation." Also included is a biography of various people you may or not be familiar with that continue to be an inspiration to me and countless students. In addition, there is a "mini-dictionary" which will assist you in expanding your vocabulary. According to the experts, the average American only adds five words a year to their vocabulary. You should be adding that many per week. And while it may not be fair, the words we choose in conversation reflect our level of education and knowledge and can be very positive, or devastating. Finally, there is a recommended reading list of books and tapes that will assist your self-enlightening journey.

Remember, the people who are successful in life do what the majority of the population refuses to do. Also, age has nothing to do with your potential however, determination does. Yesterday is history. Tomorrow is a mystery. Today is a gift. That's why it's called the present! *Excelsior: Upward & Onward.*

The power of self-affirmation centers on these three words:

YES I CAN!

These are the most important words you can say to yourself. They are supported with this statement:

"IF YOU CANNOT WIN WITH TALENT, TRIUMPH WITH EF-FORT!"

In other words, believing in yourself begins with self-confidence followed by self-esteem. It is a sad but true fact that most Americans "live a life of quiet desperation." If you are traveling through life wanting what others have and screaming, "It's not fair!" then get set for disappointment and a pessimistic self-view. But if you desire to make a difference, to make a statement with your life by developing a philosophy of life, then this book will speed you on your way.

The greatest personal affirmation statement ever uncovered comes from the Bible, passed down through the centuries, never changing in meaning. "As a man thinks in his heart, so is he." Rephrased, "As I think I am." The simple fact is that either you believe you will be successful or you believe you will not be successful. Either way, you are correct.

Nelson Mandela is a perfect example of this. He spent a better part of 28 years in a political prison in South Africa. Long after his release, numerous dignitaries from all over the world made the long trek to South Africa to meet with Mandela. Following their visits, many remarked on Mandela's astounding intelligence, wise expertise, encompassing worldview, and strong convictions. Here's why: what do you think he did for 28 years in prison? He read. He read everything he could and while doing so, believed in himself. You see, most of us believe we have problems when in all actuality, they are simply inconveniences. In 1993, Mandela and then-President of South Africa, F.W. deKlerk, were awarded the Nobel Prize for their combined efforts in abolishing apartheid, the racial segregation that ripped apart the nation. The following year, Mandela was elected as President of South Africa. His imprisonment at Robben Island, off the South tip of Cape Town, is now called "Mandela University."

The power of self-affirmation—knowing who you are and what you are capable of—is powerful indeed. The greatest waste in the world today is not the environment, it is HUMAN POTENTIAL! Millions upon millions of people sit, waiting around for "something good to happen to them." Robert Schuller perhaps said it best with his book, *If It's Going to Be, It's Up to Me.* Correct!

This brings to mind a story which has been an inspiration to countless students as well as the writer. It is the story of Maxcy Filer. Working his way through college and later through law school, he took the bar exam at the age of thirty-six. Bad news: he failed. He took it again, when his children were in grade school, and several more times while they were in high school. He failed, and failed, repeatedly. He took the bar exam in Los Angeles, San Diego, Riverside, San Francisco, anywhere in California where it was given. He continued to take the bar when his children went to college, and all throughout their years there. He continued to fail over and over again. Maxcy Filer was becoming a legend and a symbol for defeat. Not swayed, Filer again took the bar exam even when he went to work as a law clerk in his son's law practice. He failed. 47 times in all, Maxcy Filer flunked the California Bar

Exam, and then, on the 48th try, HE PASSED! After 25 years and $50,000 in fees for exams and countless review courses and a total of 144 days spent in testing rooms, he passed! He was 61 years old.

One thing Maxcy Filer knew in his heart was that he wanted to be a lawyer, and today he is. Half a mile from the courthouse in Compton, California, Maxcy Filer practices law and tells his clients, "I will fight your case to the bitter end." What do you think? I, for one, have no trouble at all believing him![1]

The following words should be pasted on your mirror, your refrigerator, your dashboard in the car, your personal space at work, your locker at school, your dorm room, and anywhere else you can view it daily:

YES I CAN!
ENDEAVOR TO PERSEVERE!

The power of self-affirmation is a personal journey. No one can do it for you. It is what you do for you through reading and consequently, education, the pursuit of knowledge, and a wider view of the world surrounding you. May you be blessed in your efforts. You can succeed and you will! Always remember:

IF YOU CANNOT WIN WITH TALENT, TRIUMPH WITH EF-FORT!

September 26, 2000

Dear Professor Mac Allen:

I was truly touched and humbled to receive your letter of congratulations dated September 17, 2000. Let me just say that I hope you and your students are not actually "amazed" by my persistence in taking the California Bar Examination. Rather, I would point out that all of us have dreams and goals to which we aspire. My dream was to be an attorney and practice law in California. Simply put, in order to practice law, you have to pass the bar examination.

Still, I would be remiss if I did not acknowledge the support and encouragement which made my dream come true. First, my wife worked several jobs and took care of the children so that I could take time off to study and prepare for the bar each time! My family always encouraged me to send in my application and "take it again!"—never once suggesting that I should give up.

Similarly, I have had a public life of political, civic and community activities here in Compton. The citizens, my neighbors and colleagues all knew of my pursuit and I could literally feel their support over the years as I biennially left for three days to take "the test."

It's not unusual for me to go into a courtroom, and the judge looks at me and says…"I took the bar with you!" As my sons would say to this…"in 24 years and 48 times…every practicing attorney in Los Angeles took the bar with you!"

I have been asked if I was embarrassed by the "failures" or because I have two sons who passed the bar before I did? My response is a resounding NO! I am proud that all of my children are pursuing their dreams. My greatest joy is witnessing their accomplishments knowing that I in some way helped lay their foundation. Plus, I have many times pointed out that "I passed the bar examination every time…*they* just didn't pass me."

In closing, I would only ask your students to pursue their individual dreams. It's never too early and it's never too late. My personal mantra was a famous quote from Winston Churchill—"Never, ever give up!" Please pass on my sincere regards and thanks to your students.

Sincerely,
Maxcy D. Filer

People succeed for two reasons:

They either wanted to prove something
or
Disprove something

DUTY

DISICIPLINE

DETERMINATION

Chapter One

*People Improve When They
Have a Reason to*

The one maxim from the Bible that has passed through the centuries and has never changed in meaning is indelibly etched as the greatest of all "winning attitude" statements: "As a man thinks in his heart, so is he." In other words, "As I think, I am."

We must always remember that we have a choice. In life, winners do the things that the majority of people refuse to do. Winners choose to wake up in the morning and go to work or to class, and choose to improve their condition in life. On the other hand, the choice is available to go on welfare, to stay in bed, to attempt to beat the Internal Revenue Service, to stay single, to let everyone else go to church. Marketers so often advise businesses, "The customer always has a choice." Dr. Denis Waitley correctly states, "Losers let it happen; winners make it happen."

Life is a do-it-with-God, do-it-for-others, do-it-for-yourself program. We are never more at our best when we are giving of ourselves; giving of ourselves is quite simply, love. Doesn't it just make perfect sense to be the best you can be when giving of yourself? Remember the three most important words we can say to ourselves are: "**YES I CAN!**" The greatest risk in life is to do nothing. If we do not decide what is important in our own lives we will most likely end up doing only the things that are important to others.

You should know if you don't already, that reading is the quickest way to knowledge. The first thing the Romans did when they entered the gates of Alexandria was to burn to the ground the greatest library the world had ever known. They knew, of course, that an educated society was a dangerous society. When Mao Tse Tung came to power in China, one of the first things he set about to do was close not just a few, but all, of the universities. No doubt for the same reason the Romans burnt Alexandria's entire library.

As Waitley points out in his book, *Seeds of Greatness*, only five percent of the people living in the United States will either buy a book or read one this year.[2] Thomas Wolfe summed it up in *The Web and the Rock*, "If we have a talent and cannot use it, we have failed. If we have a talent and use only half of it, we have partly failed. If we have a talent and learn somehow to use all of it, we have gloriously succeeded and won a satisfaction and triumph few individuals ever know."

Indeed, the possibilities are truly limitless, as Jesus stated, "All things are possible to him that believes" (Mark 9:23). Our potential is really unlimited because we serve an unlimited God. We must step out and begin to "learn for ourselves." As Mark Twain put it, "A man who picks up a cat by the tail learns something about a cat he can find out no other way." Yes! Find out for yourself. Unless you are an eyewitness, you are a false witness. Caution: one of the biggest lies of the enemy is that "I don't have time to devote to this." Satan will use this on us again and again until we believe it. One of the advantages of my graduate education was to be in a class with one of the brightest professors in the university itself. One afternoon, one of those students asked him straight away, "Dr. Williams, how did you get to be so smart?" He smiled with a downward cast in his eye for such a poorly phrased question and said, "When I was a freshman in college, I made myself a promise that I would read for fours hours each day. I would read something, anything, and here I am today to tell you that I have never broken that promise." Dr. Williams at that time was in his late seventies.

Complete silence fell on the classroom and I could hear the silent questions we all had at that moment. We all learned a priceless lesson that day—that reading is not only valuable, it is required if we are going to have a chance in life at all.

It has been proven over and over that the more education one has, the happier one is. This should be chiseled over the entry of every college and university and secondary school in America.

Today, however, our life is inundated with information so overwhelming that we hardly have time to catch our breath. For example, we live in a culture which has 260,000 billboards, 17,000 newspapers, 12,000 periodicals, 27,000 video outlets for renting videotapes, 400 million television sets, and well over 500 million radios, not including those in automobiles. There are 40,000 new book titles published every year, and each day 41 million photographs are taken. Now, thanks to the computer, over 60 billion pieces of advertising junk mail arrive in our mailboxes every year.[3]

Once you have had a moment to contemplate all this, ponder the 1994 Carnegie Corporation Report produced by the National Center for Children in Poverty. It points out that in 1960, only five percent of our children were born to unmarried mothers. In 1990, 27 percent. In 1960, less than one percent of our children under eighteen experienced the divorce of their parents. In 1990, the figure was almost 50 percent.[4]

It also should be noted that Christians fair no better in divorce. In fact, the percentage is roughly the same. We then must take courage in the Scripture that says, "Be not conformed to this world, but be transformed by the renewing of your mind, that you may prove what is that good and acceptable and perfect will of God" (Romans 12:2).

Clearly the renewing of our mind is essential, hence the reason for this book. The renewing of the mind is an ongoing process; you are a "work in progress." This means that we must as individuals educate ourselves. While it is true that not all of us can attend a college or university, it also is true that each of us can do something individually, and as a result, educate ourselves. If we are to take up leadership positions in our culture, we must be educated not only in oral communication but in written communication as well. But before this, we must begin to explore the basic core of our knowledge. It is a fact that good readers are good writers, and good writers are good readers. Through the process of reading will come the communication skills. As the great golfer Ken Venture once put it, "The more I practice, the luckier I get."

To gain a perspective regarding our starting point, let's look at where we are in education today. What better way than Finn and Diane Ravitch's book, *What Do Our Seventeen-Year-Olds Know?*

The authors have shown that 43 percent of our high school seniors could not place World War I between 1900 and 1950. More than two-thirds did not know even know the half-century in which the Civil War took place. More than 75 percent were unable to say within twenty years when Abraham Lincoln was President.

One-third of high school students tested in 1986 did not know that the Declaration of Independence marked the American colonists' break from England. Sixty percent did not know that The Federalist Papers was written to urge ratification of the Constitution, and 40 percent could not even say approximately when the Constitution was written and ratified. Only three students in five were able to recognize a definition of the system of checks and balances that divides power among three branches of American federal government.

I venture to say that although this bodes badly for high school students, much of the same holds true for college and university students as well as the majority of adults in this nation. As the Bible states, "He that walks with the wise men shall be wise; but a companion of fools shall be destroyed" (Proverbs 13:20).

"To remain ignorant of things that happened before you were born is to remain a child," Cicero said. He added, "What is a human life worth unless it is incorporated into the lives of one's ancestors and set in an historical context?" One stage in development is knowledge and we cannot get too much of it. This is only one of the reasons others around us are so successful in their daily walk. We must also distinguish between "fame" and "success." Madonna is one, Mother Teresa the other.

THE TOP 5% CLUB

- Only 5% of the population will ever engage in any self-improvement program.
- Only 5% will ever read a non-fiction book or listen to a personal growth audiotape after graduating from high school or college.
- Only 5% of the population will ever write down any goal other than a shopping list, party list, or vacation checklist.
- Only 5% will ever reach retirement age without having to depend on the government for their basic survival needs.[5]

According to William J. Bennett, former Secretary of Education under President Ronald Reagan, a student today can obtain a Bachelor's degree from 75 percent of all American colleges and universities without having studied European history, from 72 percent without having studied American literature or history, and from 86 percent without having studied the civilizations of classical Greece and Rome.

The Labor Department estimates that up to 75 percent of the non-employed lacked the necessary skills in reading and communication. A Dunn and Bradstreet report indicates that managerial inexperience and simple ineptitude account for 90 percent of small business failures. Also, some 300 plus of the nation's largest companies operate remedial courses in math and English for entry-level workers.

According to Jonathan Kozol, author of *Illiterate America*, twenty-five million American adults cannot read the poison warnings on a can of pesticide, a letter from a child's teacher, or the front page of a daily newspaper. An additional 35 million read only at a sixth grade level. Together, these 60 million people represent more than one-third of the entire adult population.[6]

Henry David Thoreau, one of America's most popular and gifted writers of the nineteenth century, is most often quoted with this statement: "The mass of men lead lives of quiet desperation and go to the grave with the song still in them." He also wrote, "Things do not change, we change," and "To be awake is to be alive."

Over the years I have come to the realization of what one of my professors remarked one afternoon during a brief break in his class. "It is so true, you know, that the majority of your college education will be learned on your own." I most certainly did not give that statement its fullest consideration until much later in my education. What he was telling us was simply put—we do much of the reading and research on our own because of term papers, projects, and various book reports; through this process, we learn. Or we may hear a book mentioned in class, write it down, go to the library and check it out; for after all, the professor mentioned it, it must be worthwhile. I, by the way, discovered numerous readings by this method. For instance, the great biography, *The Life of Samuel Johnson, LL.D.*, by James Boswell, as well as *Man's Search For Meaning*, by Victor Frankl, just to name a couple.

So many times in life we ask God for opportunities, and He disguises them as challenges, and we believe they are beyond our capacity to perform. Remember Jesus' challenge to His disciples, who were primarily fisherman, to seize the opportunity He offered to make them "fishers of men" (Matthew 4:19). He presented a challenge disguised as an opportunity.

Allan Bloom, in his profound book, *The Closing of the American Mind*, commented, "An educated person is one who is able to resist the easy and preferred answers not because he is obstinate but because he knows others worth consideration."

The most popular word in a mother and father's vocabulary is "no." We as children hear this word more often than the other 800,000 words in the common English language. From our earliest memory, we hear "No," "No, don't do that!" "No, you can't have that!" While most of the time the "no" is for our own safety or general good, we become acutely aware of it and the word becomes an integral part of our syntax.

What about those times when we actually do something and no one told us we could not? Somehow, it just never came up prior to the event and we completed whatever it was with success. Most likely, not only were we surprised but those who we know were flabbergasted!

This brings to mind the story of Tom Dempsey, born with only half of a right foot and a deformed right hand. His parents made him only comfortably aware of his handicap. As a result, the boy did everything all the other kids did. As he grew older, Tom wanted to play football. He found that he could kick the football farther than anybody. Without ever giving a negative thought to his handicap, he begged for a chance to try out for the New Orleans Saints.

The coach was doubtful but impressed when Tom Dempsey kicked a 55-yard field goal in an exhibition game. That got him the job of regular kicker for the Saints, and in that season he scored 99 points for the team.

Then came the big moment. The stadium was packed with 66,000 fans. The ball was on the 45-yard line. There was time for only one play. The coach shouted, "Dempsey, go in and try for a field goal!"

As Tom ran onto the field, he knew his team was 63 yards from the goal posts. This would be the longest kick ever made in a regular football game; the record was set at 55 yards.

The snap of the ball was perfect. Dempsey put his foot into the ball squarely as 66,000 spectators watched breathlessly. The ball had cleared the bar by inches. The team won with a score of 19 to 17. The fans went wild, thrilled by the longest field goal ever kicked. And thrilled even more by the player with half a foot and a deformed hand!

"Unbelievable!" someone shouted, but Dempsey smiled. He remembered his parents who had always told him what he could do, not what he couldn't do. He accomplished this tremendous feat because, as he puts it, "They never told me I couldn't!"[7]

Chapter Two
*Thinking: The Under-Used,
Under-Worked Exercise*

QUOTES & QUIPS ABOUT EDUCATION

"Why do Americans look up to education and look down
upon educated people?"
-Sydney J. Harris

"This will never be a civilized country until we spend more money for
books than we do for chewing gum.
-Elbert Hubbard

"Freedom of inquiry, freedom of discussion, and freedom of teaching—
without these a university cannot exist."
-Robert Maynard Hutchins

"To remain ignorant of what happened before you were born
is to remain always a child."
-Marcus Tullius Cicero

"Real education must ultimately be limited to men who insist on
knowing, the rest is mere shepherding."
-Ezra Pound

"Creative minds always have been known to survive any
kind of bad training."
-Anna Frued

"The two most common elements in the known universe
are hydrogen and stupidity."
-Harlan Ellison

"An intellectual is someone who can listen to the 'William Tell Overture'
without thinking of the Lone Ranger.
-John Chesson

"Lack of education is an extraordinary handicap
when one is being offensive."
-Josephine Tey

"Much knowledge does not teach wisdom."
-Heraclitus

"The mediocre teacher tells. The good teacher explains.
The superior teacher demonstrates. The great teacher inspires."
-William Arthur Ward

"Good teaching is one-fourth preparation and three-fourths theater."
-Gail Godwin

"Our job [teaching] is not to make up anybody's mind, but to open minds
and to make the agony of the decision-making so
intense you can only escape by thinking."
-Fred Friendly

"To teach is to learn twice."
-Joseph Joubert

"A liberal-arts education is supposed to provide you with
a value system, a standard, a set of ideas, not a job."
-Caroline Bird

"Greater is he that is in you than he that is in the world" (I John 4:4)

Most of the time we confuse a "problem" with nothing more than an inconvenience. A man who cannot find his socks and is forced to leave his house without them does not have a problem. A man with no feet has a problem. The man without socks has only an inconvenience. Once we begin to discover the maxim that says we must have information to make rational decisions, we have begun to understand the hard and cold facts that we are lacking in many areas. As James Thurber once commented, "So much has been written about everything that you can't find out anything about it." The challenge we face is obtaining the "right" information; this will challenge us long into the future.

However, in this microwave society, 30 seconds is too long. We must begin to develop the ability to be slow in well-doing. The changes through educational reading will take place gradually. Even the so-called "naturally gifted" practice for years to hone their techniques. As Margery Williams wrote in *The Velveteen Rabbit*:

"What is REAL?" asked the Rabbit one day.

"Real isn't how you are made," said the Skinhorse. "It's a thing that happens to you."

"Does it hurt?" asked the Rabbit.

"Sometimes," said the Skinhorse, for he was always truthful. "When you are real you don't mind being hurt."

"Does it happen all at once, or bit by bit?"

"It doesn't happen all at once," said the Skinhorse. "You become."

I've always been impressed with IBM and their approach to business and success, built around one word, which is their mission statement. It is simply THINK. One will see it placed in every nook and cranny of their offices—THINK!

I am not at all sure if this story is true, however, I like to believe it is. One afternoon, three astronauts were asked separately, "If you had ten seconds to live, what would you do?" All three answered the same: "I would take nine seconds to think about it."

Thinking is the basis of an education, whether we obtain it through formal instruction or on our own. And because you are reading this book, you obviously feel the need to do something on your own or for others. As Emerson said, "The things taught in schools and colleges are not an education, but the means of education."

Horace Mann put it this way, "Keep one thing forever in view: the truth;

and if you do this, though it may seem to lead you away from the opinions of men, it will assuredly conduct you to the throne of God."

One of my former colleagues tells the story of one of his students who made a zero on a semester final. More than just a little put out, he made an appointment to see the professor and said, "I do not think I deserve a zero."

"Neither do I," declared the professor, "but it's the lowest grade I could give you!"

More times than not, we attempt to do it ourselves with an ability we only "think" we possess. We might not always have the solution, but we are never absolved from the responsibility of trying. Success is not the measure, effort is.

As the Scripture tells us, "Trust in the Lord with all your heart; lean not on your own understanding. Be not wise in your own eyes" (Proverbs 3:5,7). "The way of a fool is right in his own eyes; but he that harkens unto counsel is wise" (Proverbs 12:15). And, "No doubt but you are the people, and wisdom shall die with you" (Job 12:2).

Therefore, it goes without saying that wisdom and the obtaining therein takes effort and time, and is, in general, a slow process. "If you cry after knowledge, and lift up your voice for understanding; if you seek her as silver, and search for her as for hidden treasures, then shall you understand the fear of the Lord, and find knowledge of God" (Proverbs 2:3-5).

How many people have you known who say, "I know I worry too much, but I can't help it," or who live by the maxim, "What if?" Worry can be the demise of us all if we let it take control; so before you embark on your self-education, let us dispel the "myth of worry."

Experts have estimated that of all the things we worry about, 40 percent will never happen; 30 percent are past, and all the worry in the world cannot change them; 12 percent are needless worries about our health; 10 percent are petty, miscellaneous worries; leaving 8 percent for things that legitimately deserve our concern and thought. This means that 92 percent of the things you worry about, if you tend to be something of a worrier, will never happen. They are either in the past or do not deserve your attention.[8]

A man by the name of M J Savage put it in the right perspective when he said: "If any young person expects, without faith, without study, without patient and persevering labor, in the midst of and in spite of discouragement, to attain anything in this world that is worth attaining, they will simply wake up by and by and find that they have been playing the part of a fool."[9]

The Master Word, written by the great physician Sir William Osler, is about a word that could wipe out welfare as we know it in this nation. It is a word that will bring satisfaction, clarity, stability, self-respect, and self-confidence to our lives. As Dr. Osler puts it, "Though little, the master word looms large in meaning. It is the "open sesame" to every portal, the great equalizer, the philosopher's stone that transmutes all the basic metal of humanity into gold. The stupid it will make bright, the bright, brilliant, and the brilliant, steady. To youth it brings hope, to the middle-aged, confidence, to the aged, repose.

Do you know what that word is? It is WORK![10]

I teach all my students: "Be yourself, there's nobody more qualified." It is a sad but true fact that most of us are trying to be somebody else, to do things like those we either know or have heard about. In actuality, if we would just be ourselves as God intended, most of our troubles in life would come into perspective.

We must take initiative in life and utilize all of our strengths, especially those which the Creator has given us, and use these to not only better the life of ourselves, but also those around us and those we have yet to meet. My father told me as a young boy to "plant a tree under which you will never sit to enjoy the shade." He was also fond of saying, "We are here to help others. What others are doing, I have no idea." Perhaps we're not really supposed to know!

However, this is one thing we do know, if we can read and do not, we are no better off than someone who cannot read at all. This should also be chiseled in stone above every school, college, and university in America. While, according to the American Booksellers Association, 90% of the population is able to read, only about 25 percent buy books. If you doubt this, take a trip this weekend to any national bookseller and observe those in the store. This will be easy to accomplish because the aisles will be mostly empty. Remember, we are authorized to think and equipped with the proper information, we should be able to use our own best judgment at all times. People are at their best when they have an opportunity to change the way things appear to be in life. And do not forget the management cliché: "What gets rewarded gets done." Mediocrity is expensive. As we begin to explore the great works of history and individual effort, our insight will begin to develop greatly, and we will begin to see things differently. The world around us will come into a new light. "I said, I will be wise, but it was far from me. That which is far off, and exceedingly deep, who can find it out?" (Ecclesiastes 7:23, 24).

If we were to ask who was the first person to climb Mount Everest, the highest mountain in the world, we would find that the majority of those asked would be lost to find an answer. The first person to ever conquer the mighty mountain was Sir Edmond Hillary; however, he did not succeed in his first attempt. In fact, two climbers were left behind on the snow-covered slopes. When he returned home he was given a special dinner and a banquet in his honor, following being knighted by the queen. At the reception there was a huge picture of Mount Everest behind the podium. Following a glowing introduction Hillary walked to the lectern, turned and looked at the picture, pointing his finger and saying, "Mount Everest, you can't get any bigger, but I can!"[11]

As General George Patton so aptly stated, "I don't care how smart you are or what gifted talents you have, if you don't have this, you will fail as a leader, no matter how hard you try." The "this" he was speaking of is self-confidence. We must have self-confidence no matter what we are attempting to do. Self-confidence says, "I'm ready. I can do this. I have enough ability in myself to know I can." In fact, it is this self-talk that will convince us of our ability and will provide the catalyst to victory.

As Daniel Webster said, "if we work marble, it will perish; if we work upon brass, time will efface it; if we rear temples, they will crumble into dust; but if we work upon immortal minds and instill in them just principles, we are engraving upon tablets which no time will efface, but will brighten and brighten to all eternity."

Self-education is a task and while this text is by no means a definitive work on education, it is a beginning; it is a test. As a mother once said, "We ask for strength, and God gives us difficulties which make us strong. We plead for courage, and God gives us danger to overcome. We ask for favors, and God gives us opportunities. We pray for happiness, and God gives us challenges to test our faith."

True, education cannot make us all leaders, but it can teach us which leaders to follow. Education is not perceived, it is achieved, and curiosity in many instances is the key to success. Thus, be perpetually curious!

The deciding difference in today's world is information. To prove ourselves in society we must learn to develop a winning attitude by first learning to resist complacency. We should refuse to be satisfied with what we know now and covet knowledge. We must develop integrity, vision, and self-discipline. Remember the recipe for ignorance: "Be satisfied with your opinions and content with your knowledge."

With computer technology as prevalent as it is today, we might believe that everything we could possibly learn is right in front of us, on the screen. Why bother with books, the library, and reason? A good question, to be sure, but one that needs further exploring. For example, take the situation that occurred in the 1930s. American chicken hatchers faced a problem that threatened to literally destroy their industry. Their very survival depended upon a way to tell the difference between female chicks—which were sold for profit as layers—and male chicks—most of which were worthless in the profit column. The obvious solution, such as waiting to maturity, was economically unfeasible.

Willing to attempt anything at this point, the industry heard about a group in Japan called "chick sexors." So they brought in five of these people. To their surprise, one of the five, Hikosoboro Yogo, proved able to accurately "sex" 1400, one-day-old chicks per hour with 98 percent accuracy.

"Oddly, Yogo selected the female chicks without even looking at their sex organs. After handling three to four million chicks, he just seemed to know which was which. Further, he could not really explain how he did it. Fortunately for the poultry industry, American chicken sexors were able to pick up his uncanny skill by watching him for three months."[12]

Hurbert and Stuart Dreyfus, in Mind Over Machine (Free Press), argue that Yogo's expertise is precisely the sort that machines, including computers, will never—that's never—attain. They conclude that the goal of trying to make computers work out solutions to problems the way human experts do is both a philosophical and a practical impossibility.

This underscores the very basic premise I attempt to teach my students each day, that there is more to a college degree than sitting in class. To survive a lifetime we must all learn how to learn, to adapt, to lead. These are lessons that only can be learned by involving ourselves in a total self-absorbing learning experience.

For example, students who drive to campus, go to class, and then go home are wasting their time and money. What is worse than this scenario is the students who sit in front of a computer or watch videos to obtain their degree. They are taking the path of least resistance from present mediocrity to future mediocrity. Always remember, the room for improvement is the largest room in the world. As Percy W. Bridgeman said, "There are techniques of being intelligent. It is not easy to acquire the proper use of mental tools that we have thoughtlessly inherited or which are implicit in the construction of our brains. Severe effort and long practice are required."

If we take up the challenge of books and other instructional suggestions, I can say with complete confidence that we will know a great deal more than the average college graduate, and as much or more as those in graduate school studies. Why? Quite simply, the majority of colleges and universities today do not require of their students the rigorous task of "reading" anything other than rote and boring textbooks. As Jacob Bronowski puts it: "Knowledge is not a loose-leaf notebook of facts. It is the responsibility for the integrity of what we are. You cannot possibly maintain that informed integrity if you let other people run the world for you, while you yourself continue to live out of a ragbag or worn-out information from old beliefs."[13]

Chapter Three
Knowledge: The Individual Quest

"Apply thine heart unto instruction, and thine ears to the words of knowledge. Buy the truth and sell it not; also wisdom and instruction, and understanding" (Proverbs 23:12, 23).

One of the myths that we humans seem to lean on like a crutch is that we must always learn from someone else. Nothing could be farther from the truth. While this may be an optimum way to learn—seeing something done, being told something, then demonstrated by example—we must take it upon ourselves personally to seek knowledge as an individual quest.

And, with the "political correctness" of our time (I have yet to hear the politically correct way to refer to a manhole cover…), we can and will become confused. For example, hospitals today do not record a death in their facilities; they have what is called a "negative patient outcome." Come on, the person died! Just be truthful. We attempt to cover up certain aspects of our daily lives by bloating the language; after all, it sounds "correct."

It has also become evident that our schools can no longer be trusted with the education of our children. We must take control in the home to provide the best education possible for our children; the finished product is our future.

The public's complacency with the sad commentary of our educational system demands accountability. Sixty-three percent of those ages 18 to 24 cannot find France on an unlabeled map (fewer than half find New York); 60 percent of high school juniors do not know why the Federalist Papers were written; in tests comparing the math and science skills of thirteen-year-old Americans with those of five other countries and four Canadian provinces, our nation finished last. We most assuredly become alarmed at facts such as these and it continues to get worse. New York Telephone finds that 115,000 of 117,000 applicants flunk its employment exam; 80 percent of applicants flunk Motorola's exam seeking levels of seventh-grade English and fifth-grade math.[14]

Epictetus, the first century Greek philosopher, said, "Practice yourself, for heaven's sake, in little things; and thence proceed to greater." Another of his famous quotations is, "It is not what happens to you but how you react to it that matters." Perhaps one of my favorites is from Goethe and is on a wall plaque at the Naval War College: "There is nothing more terrifying than ignorance in action."

We are all students of life and are very much aware that people will listen to and understand only as much as they are willing to incorporate into their own thinking. Let it be said that minds are like parachutes; they work best when they are open.

Sir Hugh Rigby, surgeon to King George IV, was once asked what makes a great surgeon. He replied, "I do not believe it is necessarily manual dexterity; I rather believe that some just know more than others." Absolutely correct—in most if not all professions, some people do just know more than others and age has little or nothing to do with it. The more knowledgeable are, in fact, those people who work harder, study longer, and internalize information better by rehearsing each day to take in as much as they can hold. As former Congressman Bill Bradley once remarked about his National Basketball Association career, "If you are not practicing every day, someday you will meet a man who is, and when you do, he will win."

In my Army days our platoon sergeant would remind us at least three times a week, "Problems we can deal with, it's habits that bring us the real trouble." According to neurophysiologist Mortimer Mishkin, habit is one of two distinct systems of learning we possess. The first system is rational, conscious, and cognitive, and takes place in the limbic structures of the brain. This is learning by knowing something. The other system, habit, is based on simple repetition. Mishkin believes it takes place in the striature, one of the brain's most primitive areas, and he comments in an issue of the Scientific American that "habit is founded not on knowledge or even memories . . . but on automatic connections between stimulus and response."

Therefore, a "habit" of seeking knowledge will continue to reinforce our worth not only to ourselves but to the world around us. As Goethe said, "If you treat an individual as he is, he will stay that way, but if you treat him as if he were what he could be, he will become what he could be." Treat yourself as what you can be—intelligent, informed, and confident in your knowledge—and you will become that person.

We should be extremely concerned with the rising tide of mediocrity and take it upon ourselves to make sure it does not reach us personally. We must do everything in our power to become friends to the past through historical record, friends to today in order to make rational decisions, and friends to the future based on collective knowledge. When we are right, reassure; when we are wrong, learn. Education will do this for us while maintaining our integrity and self-confidence. This self-assurance will indeed open many new vistas in our lives. As a wise man once said, "The deepest principle of human nature is the craving to be appreciated." The exact opposite of being appreciated is having others laugh at you. In fact, among the Native Alaskan people, laughter is the only punishment for thieves. If a person is found to be a thief, all the people of the village laugh at him whenever they see him. As a result there is very little thievery among the Eskimos.[15]

Taking responsibility for our own education is most certainly nothing new. It is done each day. All of life is continuing education; and put simply, we never stop learning. Even if we wanted to stop learning, we couldn't. In this process, this self-education, we are taking personal and political responsibility for our own lives. We will be the same today as we will be five years from today, with two exceptions: the books we read and the people we meet. Neil Postman in *Conscientious Objections*, puts our situation this way:

> When a culture becomes overloaded with pictures; when logic and rhetoric lose their binding authority; when historical truth becomes irrelevant; when the spoken word is distrusted or makes demands on our attention so that we are incapable of giving; when our politics, history, education, religion, public information, and commerce are expressed in visual imagery rather than words, then a culture is in serious jeopardy.[16]

It is said that someone once asked Helen Keller to identify the worst thing that could happen to a person. "The worst thing," she replied, "is to have vision and not see."

"The just man walks in his integrity; his children are blessed after him" (Proverbs 20:7). And so, be designed to look at life as an accomplishment and consider the following suggestions:

- **Today is a day for accomplishment in my personal development. I will devote the time it takes as well as the effort.**

- **I will set a goal each day for this accomplishment, and then I will go at least 10 percent above it each day. For example, if I plan to read and study for two hours, I will then go beyond that by twelve minutes.**
- **I will write down in pen or pencil what I want to remember and if I want to make it a part of my internalization of information, I will write it again and again until it becomes permanent.**

- **I will not let anything or anyone discourage me from my daily accomplishment.**

- **I will say what I do…and I will do what I say. This is a promise I will make to myself each day and I will live up to it.**

In his book, *Meditation*, author Eknath Easwaran advises that we spend at least thirty minutes each day in meditation, repeating the prayer of St. Francis. This will lay the foundation for your daily accomplishment.

The Prayer of St. Francis of Assisi

Lord, make me an instrument of thy peace.
Where there is hatred, let me sow love;
Where there is injury, pardon;
Where there is doubt, faith;
Where there is despair, hope;
Where there is darkness, light;
Where there is sadness, joy.

O divine Master, grant me that I may not so much seek
To be consoled as to console
To be understood as to understand,
To be loved as to love.
For it is in giving that we receive;
It is in the pardoning that we are pardoned;
It is in the dying to self that we are born to eternal life.[17]

The Chinese philosopher Seng T'san offers this wisdom: "Stop talking, stop thinking, and there is nothing you will not understand." As you begin to investigate "the classics," as we have come to know them, you will almost instantly become aware of the world around you and the daily events that make up our so-called "news of the day." Is this important, this daily excursion into the wicked world of events? It is more than important; it is essential. If more Christians were to "tune in" we would not have Roe v. Wade as our country's mandate, nor would Jesus and God be barred from our nation's schools, replaced by condoms. While it is true that publications such as *Time* and *Newsweek* are extremely liberal in their news approach, this does not relieve us from the responsibility to learn their agenda. One of the main complaints I receive from employers about our students these days is that they are not well informed of the world around them. This is especially true in Christian schools, but is not exclusive. We simply have to do a better job in preparation. Educators should require a very basic civics lesson daily, be they secondary school teachers or college professors. I can recall my experience with one particular college president who each Monday morning in our weekly meeting would ask, "What are you reading this week?" Perhaps this idea should be transformed into the family discussion each week. This could only have a tremendous and positive effect on the learning curve in America.

Today we hear the phrase, "the dumbing down of America." For most of us it is more than just a phrase; it is reality. What began once as a basic course, such as English—which was not a subject in American schools until the 1920s—has now been turned into a hybrid under so many names one cannot discern them from college catalog to college catalog. The ancient Greeks had a curriculum formed around the study of "harmonics," and thus today we have math, astronomy, music, and geometry lumped together. The Sophists placed great value on grammar, logic, and rhetoric. Plato, for example, thought logic should not be attempted until one reached the age of thirty-five.[18]

Always an intriguing passage, former President James Madison wrote in Federalist Paper No. 49: "A reverence for the laws would be sufficiently inculcated by the voice of an enlightened person."[19] And Thomas Jefferson closed one of his letters to Madison with, "The education of the common people will be attended to; convinced that on their good sense we may rely with the most security for the preservation of a due degree of liberty." And some twenty-eight years later he added, "The diffusion of knowledge is the only guardian of true liberty."[20]

"And are confident that thou thyself are a guide of the blind, a light of them which are in darkness, an instructor of the foolish, a teacher of the truth in the law" (Romans 2:19,20).

Being advised as to what your government is doing in general and personally is in and of itself an education and thus presents the absolute need for you to be informed. As J. Peter Grace, chief executive officer of the W.R. Grace Company says:

> Here's the apple. My generation has already taken a bite out of
> it. But, like Adam, you have to make the best of an imperfect
> garden. What can you do? Two things: continue to learn and be
> sure to vote. First, learn. Inform yourselves. Read and think.

Don't swallow what others say. Reflect continually about your government and who is running it because they will be doing it with your money. Second, vote . . . because how can you correct the follies of my generation unless you vote against them.[21]

For many of us our lives are cities with only suburbs and we lack a certain continuity to explain it all. For some of us the church may add its wisdom, but overall, studies such as psychology, sociology, history, and biology are what we will eventually turn to for answers. After all, our moral consequences are at stake here, and knowledge, both of alternative sources of actions and clarification of such consequences, depends upon it. "Education, then, beyond all other devices of human origin," declared Horace Mann, "is the great equalizer of the conditions of men." Knowledge is liberty and ignorance is captivity. Knowledge will break the bondage that keeps you from advancing.

- **A man of knowledge increases his learning and "shall attain unto wise counsel" (Proverbs 1:5).**

- **"Fools hate knowledge" (Proverbs 1:22). Some say that is why they are fools.**

- **"The ears of the wise seek knowledge" (Proverbs 18:15).**

- **"The lips of knowledge are a precious jewel" (Proverbs 20:15).**

- **"A wise man is strong; yea, a man of knowledge increases strength" (Proverbs 24:5).**

- **"The excellency of knowledge is that wisdom gives life to them that have it" (Ecclesiastes 7:12).**

If you are to make the most of your life then you must lead yourself and others as the Holy Spirit recommends and you must know that you know.

> "He who knows, and knows he knows—
> He is wise—follow him."
> --Arabian Proverb

As Alfred North Whitehead stated so correctly, "The best education is to be found in gaining the utmost information from the simplest apparatus."

One of our wisest founding fathers, James Madison, wrote, "A people who mean to be their own governors must arm themselves with the power knowledge gives. A popular government without popular information or the means of acquiring it is but a prologue to a farce or a tragedy, or perhaps both."

The clear task before us all is as the Roman orator-poet-statesman Cicero observed: "Nature has planted in our minds an insatiable longing to see the truth." This is what we are beginning to do now. It is said that we should not worry about the things we do not know. What leads us into trouble are the things we know for sure that are not so!

Basically, there are two branches of logic: epistemology, which discusses the nature of truth and certain knowledge of truth; and dialectics, which are the correct ways of thinking in order that we may reach the truth. Dialectics consists of three main operations of intellect: 1) simple comprehension; 2) judgment; 3) reasoning.

Simple comprehension merely means the grasping or seizing by the mind of an object or thing—being aware of it and going no further. On the other hand, if we think, "This is a round fruit," we would be going into judgment. In order to reach the judgment stage, two simple comprehensions pertaining to the same subject are necessary. First by using the fruit, one simple comprehension is the fact that the object is fruit; the second simple comprehension is that it is round. This leads back to the judgment, "This is a round fruit." Just as judgment needs two simple comprehensions, two judgments are necessary to become reasoning. Note the following example:

1) This is a good book. (First judgment)
2) I like reading this book. (Second judgment)
3) Therefore, I like books. (Reasoning or conclusion)

Although there are two kinds of reasoning—induction (inductive) and deduction (deductive)—we will only discuss deduction, and at that, a small part. Now enter the word syllogism: "A deductive scheme of a formal argument consisting of a major and a minor premise and a conclusion." This is a form of thinking that we do almost every day without even realizing the process. It is a form of thinking that can and very often does lead us away from the path of truth. The following is an example of a syllogism:

1) All men are mortal.
2) Socrates is a man.
3) Therefore, Socrates is mortal.

The mistake lies in the use of applying an instance to prove a generalization and the most common error of substituting "all" for "some." An example follows:

1) Soups are always served hot.
2) Vichyssoise is a soup.
3) Therefore, vichyssoise is always served hot.

The reasoning in this example is fine, yet the conclusion is incorrect simply because the original premise—the starting point of thinking—is false. Soups are NOT always served hot; and, as a matter of fact, vichyssoise is served cold. This type of syllogism is prejudging; making up our minds about a class of things from one instance.

Remember, the syllogistic way of thinking brings people illogically to the conclusion hoped for by various advertisers, politicians, news reporters, talk show hosts and panels, and speech makers, in large part. Note the following example:

1) Joe Jones is a very famous personality.
2) Joe Jones uses Brand X soap.
3) Therefore, Brand X soap must be very good soap.

Remember, clear thinking should become a part of our daily lives. Look and listen before taking syllogism for granted. God gave us two ears and one mouth; we should use them accordingly. Let us also remember some people believe that facts are like cows: If we look them in the face hard enough, they generally run away.

Thinking is difficult and takes concentration and devotion to reach the goal of solutions. This brings to mind the story of the German Army in World War II. At the end of the war, the Allies found records of every commissioned officer in the German ranks. The record detailed the battles in which each officer fought and what he did. Each contained a shorthand code that described the officer as either S & L, B & I, S & I, or B & L. The Allies discovered that "B" stood for brilliant, "S" for stupid, "I" for industrious, and "L" for lazy.

Matching these classifications against the officers' war records showed, surprisingly, that those labeled brilliant and industrious were good field officers, and the stupid and lazy were bad ones. The stupid and industrious proved disastrous; they had little idea what they were doing but worked constantly to do it. The most successful group included the brilliant and lazy. They were the planners and innovators, the real brains of the army. They created rockets and other new forms of weaponry that made the Germans so hard to beat. Even during the stressful days of the war, they took the time to think about how to carry on.

The moral of this story is that neither brilliance nor fanatical dedication is enough to carry you to the top. Action for its own sake even can do more harm than good. The person who spends serious time thinking will rise to the top with an easier, better way to accomplish his or her goals.[22]

As we gain knowledge and begin to apply it in daily life, we will soon discover the difference between obstacles and opportunities. Many years ago, a large American shoe manufacturer sent two sales reps out to different parts of the Australian outback to see if they could drum up some business among the aborigines. Some time later, the company received telegrams from both agents.

The first one said, "No business here. Natives don't wear shoes."

The second one said, "Great opportunity here—natives don't wear shoes!"[23]

Thinking and learning takes time. There are 10,080 minutes in a week or 168 hours. This is our wealth in time. What we spend it on is our choice, but no matter what, we never get more than 10,080 minutes or 168 hours per week. Now, put our time together with the 800,000 or so words in the English language—of which the average person will use approximately 800—and compound that with these words having some 14,000 meanings in total, and we have an interpreting difficulty in just how these words were intended.

While this may seem overwhelming, it isn't. The best time to begin our information review and learning experience is now. In the well-known "Shoe" comic strip, the leading character says, "I try to set aside one day each week and devote it entirely to my work."

"That's a good idea," responded a friend. "What day of the week is that for you?"

"Tomorrow," is his answer.

"Experience tells you what to do; confidence allows you to do it."
-Stan Smith

In 1999, South African President Nelson Mandela celebrated his eightieth birthday.

For almost 26 of those years, he was confined to a prison cell because of his outspoken views about apartheid. During this time, Mandela's confidence must have been severely tested. It is a tribute to his faith and conviction that he ultimately triumphed and went on to be elected to his country's highest office.

Confidence is a habit that can be honed and strengthened every day. During this process you will be challenged by fear, worry and uncertainty. These elements constitute the ebb and flow of life. It's a constant struggle, a mental battlefield that must be won if your life is to be filled with abundance. To start, carefully read the words spoken by Nelson Mandela at his inaugural speech. This is a man who accepted challenge and won. Digest each sentence slowly. Use them as a foundation for your next level of achievement.

Our deepest fear is not that we are inadequate.

Our deepest fear is that we are powerful beyond measure.
It is our light, not our darkness that frightens us.

We ask ourselves, who am I to be brilliant, gorgeous, talented and fabulous?

Actually, who are we not to be?

You are a child of God.

Your playing small doesn't serve the world.

There's nothing enlightened about shrinking so that other people won't feel insecure around you.

We were born to make manifest the glory of God that is within us.

It's not just in some of us, it's in everyone.

And as we let our own light shine, we unconsciously give other people permission to do the same.

As we are liberated from our own fears, our presence automatically liberates others.[24]

FIVE CONFIDENCE-BUILDING STRATEGIES

Building self-confidence is an on-going exercise and to be successful, one must practice on a daily basis. An outstanding example of the exercises you can implement is found in a wonderful book entitled: The Power of Focus by authors Jack Canfield, Mark Victor Hansen, and Les Hewitt. (Health Communications Inc.).

What follows is an excellent self-affirmation strategy:

- EVERY DAY REMIND YOURSELF THAT YOU DID THINGS WELL: Don't dwell of what didn't work or the tasks you didn't finish focus on what you did accomplish. Don't minimize these. Give yourself a pep talk at the beginning and end of the day. Coach yourself, just like you would help someone else to overcome a challenge.

- READ INSPIRING BIOGRAPHIES AND AUTOBIOGRAPHIES: Read books, articles and magazines. Build a file of those stories that inspire y you most. Record special documentaries. Listen to tapes or watch videos. Go to the movies—there are a lot of great stories out there. Find out about people who started with nothing, or who had devastating setbacks, and still found a way to win. Remember, your capacity far exceeds your current level of performance. Life without challenges is an illusion. Accept the fact that you will have ups and downs, just like everyone else. Your confidence grows when you actively take on the challenges of life. You won't win them all, but with the right attitude you'll win more than enough.

- BE THANKFUL: No matter how bad your circumstances may be, there's probably someone worse off than you. If you doubt this, volunteer your time in an acute-care burns ward at the children's hospital. Put things into perspective. Think of all the things (and people) you take for granted that are not available in other countries. Most of your problems will pale in comparison when you take a mental snapshot of all the benefits you enjoy everyday.

- PUSH YOURSELF TO ACCOMPLISH SHORT-TERM GOALS: There's no better way to build confidence than getting things done. Create an environment of accomplishment every week. Focus on your three most important targets. Every day do something that moves you closer to finishing a project or expanding a relationship. Don't allow yourself to be distracted or interrupted. By doing so you'll eliminate the feelings of guilt and failure. Take one small step at a time.

  Make sure your goals are realistic. Self-rejection can shatter your confidence; so don't beat yourself up when everything doesn't come together as planned. Be flexible. And when others say "No" to you, don't take it personally. Accept the fact that you need to lose sometimes before you can win.

- DO SOMETHING FOR YOURSELF EVERY WEEK: Find a way to celebrate your weekly accomplishments. Don't you deserve it? If you said "No," go back to step one and start again.

The road to confidence is paved with weekly victories

**"Experience tells you what to do,
confidence allows you to do it."
-Stan Smith**

(Source: *The Power of Focus* by Jack Canfield, Health Communications Inc. Deerfield Beach, Florida, 2000, pp-158, 174, 175, & 176.)

EITHER YOU BELIEVE YOU WILL BE SUCCESSFUL

OR

YOU BELIEVE YOU WON'T

BUT EITHER WAY

YOU'RE GOING TO BE RIGHT

One person with commitment, persistence, and endurance will accomplish more than a thousand people with interest alone.

In the Far East the people plant a tree called the Chinese bamboo. During the first four years they water and fertilize the plant with seemingly little or no results. The fifth year they again apply water and fertilize—and in five weeks time the tree grows 90 feet in height! The obvious question is; did the Chinese bamboo tree grow ninety feet in five weeks, or did it grow ninety feet in five years?

The answer is: it grew ninety feet in five years. Because if at any time during those five years the people had stopped watering and fertilizing the tree, it would have died.

If we don't decide what is important in our own lives, we will probably end up doing only the things that are important to others.

Take time to WORK
- it is the price of success;
Take time to PLAY
- it is the secret of perpetual youth;
Take time to THINK
- it is the source of power;
Take time to READ
- it is the fountain of wisdom;
Take time to WORSHIP
- it is the highway of reverence;
Take time to PRAY
- it is the greatest power of earth;
Take time to LISTEN
- it is the music of the soul;
Take time to DREAM
- it is the pathway to understanding;
Take time to LOVE and be LOVED
- it is the gift of God.

Author Unknown

...It's up to US.

We do not choose to be born. We do not choose our parents. We do not choose our historical epoch or the country of our birth or the immediate circumstances of our upbringing. We do not, most of us, choose to die; nor do we choose the time or conditions of our death. But within all this realm of choicelessness, we do choose how we shall live: courageously or in a cowardice, honorable or dishonorably, with purpose or adrift. We decide what is important and what is trivial in life. We decide that what makes us significant is either what we do or what we refuse to do. But no matter how indifferent the universe may be to your choices and decisions, these choices and decisions are ours to make.

We decide. We choose. And as we decide and choose so our lives are formed. In the end, forming our own destiny is what ambition is all about.[25]

We ask for strength, and God gives us difficulties which make us strong. We plead for courage, and God gives us danger to overcome. We ask for favors, and God gives us opportunities. We pray for happiness, and God gives us challenges to test our faith.

Chapter Four
Thinking and Learning Take Time

One man esteems one above another; another esteems every day alike. Let every man be fully persuaded in his own mind. To him that esteems anything to be unclean, to him it is unclean. Hast thou faith? Have it thyself before God. Happy is he that condemns not himself in that thing which he allows (Romans 14:5, 14, 22).

Until we are committed to a goal, there is a hesitancy, the chance to draw back, always ineffectiveness. Concerning all acts of initiative (and creation), one elementary truth exists, the ignorance of which kills countless ideas and splendid plans: The moment we definitely commit ourselves, then Providence moves as well. All sorts of things occur to help us that otherwise would never have occurred. A whole stream of events issues from the decision, raising in our favor all manner of unforeseen incidents and meetings and material assistance, which no man or woman could have dreamed would have come his or her way. I have learned a deep respect for one of Goethe's couplets: "Whatever you can do, or dream you can, begin it. Boldness has genius, power, and magic in it."[26]

As the great coach of Notre Dame, Lou Holtz, instructs his players: "Ability is what you're capable of doing. Motivation determines what you do. Attitude determines how well you do it." And while we may have experienced set backs in our lives before (haven't we all), just remember that history is full of people who have experienced defeat many, many times and have refocused and gone on to elaborate success. Failure is not an event, it is a matter of opinion.

Harry S. Truman, said to be one of the most effective presidents of our recent time, was elected to the United States Senate at the age of fifty and was president at sixty. As we live each day we accumulate knowledge of what has happened, what is completed, what is sure. This knowledge provides us the means to understanding and gives purpose to the events that are perplexing us each day and helps us know what should be done. In short, knowledge gives us a past experience offering us an advantage in which to look at a situation or problem in a new perspective. Some of us take longer than others to accumulate this knowledge, but as the example below points out, effect will win out in the long run:

> An excellent plumber is infinitely more admirable than an incompetent philosopher. The society that scorns excellence in plumbing because plumbing is a humble activity and tolerates shoddiness in philosophy because it is an exalted activity will

> have neither good plumbing nor good philosophy. Neither its
> pipes nor its theories will hold water.[27]
> --John Gardner

If we listen carefully today to conversations regarding the subject of role models, or people who are admired, we will hear names like Michael Jordan, Princess Diana, Tom Cruise, and perhaps even Billy Graham. Our main exposure comes, of course, from television and can be likened to total strangers worshiping total strangers. It is somehow believed that if we as individuals could just have a portion of what these role models have, we could be oh, so happy. Happiness today is so misconstrued in society; many of us believe if we could just get what we want, we would be happy—money, fame, respect, admiration, high office. Our life would be, in all reasoning, ideal. I propose that happiness is not so much getting what we want as it is not experiencing things that could have happened to us, such as a debilitating disease or the loss of a limb, or worse. In a sense, this can make us content and happy as well.

If we could take the time to search our libraries and bookstores, we would find a wealth of overcomers and achievers to emulate and soon discover how fate and circumstance can be observed. We would note the value we as a society place on superficial things and people. Edward Everett (1794–1865) was a man of great accomplishment: American statesman, orator, and scholar. Everett graduated from Harvard in 1811, and was for some time a Unitarian clergyman. He became professor of Greek at Harvard in 1815, traveled to Europe from 1815 to 1818, and was editor of the *North American Review* from 1820 to 1824. Everett was elected to Congress and served from 1836 to 1840, was governor of Massachusetts, and ambassador to the Court of St. James. Later, he became president of Harvard University and served from 1846 to 1849. He then became Secretary of State in 1852 and was elected to the United States Senate in 1853. Then in 1860 he ran for Vice-President as a candidate of the Constitutional Party. But for all of his accomplishments, he was best known for his oratory, especially in Washington, which earned him nearly $100,000. This he gave to the purchase of Mt. Vernon.[28]

Needless to say, during his life on earth, he was known for his elegant delivery, rich voice, immaculate dress, and cultured manner. His most famous and last oratorical address came November 19, 1863, at a dedication for a cemetery. When he was first invited to give the address in August, he declined due to scheduling difficulties. A date was then determined which Everett set in order to have three weeks preparation time. The organizers agreed.

Finally the day arrived and as he approached the podium he was greeted literally by hundreds of admirers and curiosity seekers hoping to just get a glimpse of the great man. He did not disappoint those attending that day, as he spoke for approximately 58 minutes from no visible notes. He returned to his seat as thundering applause surrounded the countryside. Those attending the dedication of the Gettysburg Cemetery that day also heard another speaker, the President of the United States, Abraham Lincoln, whose simpler and more moving phrases overshadowed his famous predecessor; even to this day, we hear little or nothing about the great orator Edward Everett, but rather, it is the Gettysburg Address that remains fresh in our minds.

The point here is that perspective in our lives should be investigated, not superficially; it takes searching, and thus the need for knowledge and the search for factual accounts for our own satisfaction. "Better is the poor that walks in his integrity than he that is perverse in his lips and is a fool" (Proverbs 19:1).

"To accuse others for one's misfortunes is a sigh of want of education. To accuse oneself shows that one's education has begun. To accuse neither oneself nor others shows one's education is complete," explained Epictetus.

The educator and author J.B. Matthews put it another way: "Unless a person has trained himself for his chance, the chance will only make him look ridiculous. A great occasion is worth to a man exactly what his preparation enables him to make of it."

Remember our enemy and keep ever so vigilant of him. He will steal, destroy, and take from us everything we ever hoped or dreamed of becoming. This enemy is visible daily in each of our lives and the struggle of life reveals his tactics and strategies. Who is this enemy? Ignorance and the mistaken belief that we can receive more than we actually earn on our own. Knowledge, then, is indeed power, power over ignorance; for after all, it can be demonstrated in the way we speak, perform our jobs, deal with our marriages, and in general, raise our children. Learning can and will never stop

No one person can know everything. The only person, or should I say, the last person to know everything in the world was Erasmus who lived in the 1300s. We most certainly cannot walk into the Library of Congress with its millions of volumes and begin reading, for if we lived a thousand years, we could not possibly read them all. However, our self-taught experience must begin somewhere and in that lies at least one answer, the English language. When you begin to examine various books and publications recommended in this book, you will begin to also study the language. In a *Reader's Digest* article several years ago, author Blake Clark wrote, "Tests of more than 350,000 persons from all walks of life show that, more often than any other measurable characteristic, knowledge of the exact meanings of a large number of words accompanies outstanding success." When we examine the average person in this nation, we find that he or she accumulates approximately only five words of vocabulary each year. We begin to realize the importance this exercise holds.[29]

THE DR. FOX EFFECT

The unwarranted credibility of authoritive sources is so well documented that it has received a name: the "Dr. Fox Effect."

Dr. Fox was not a doctor at all, but an actor who presented a lecture to students and faculty at a major medical school. The lecture was amusing, and it was carefully written to include contradictions and nonsense, and to avoid conveying any real information.

The audience rated the lecture on an eight-item questionnaire, and Dr. Fox's evaluations were very favorable. Remember, when sources seem authoritative, even experts grant them more credibility than they deserve.

THE THEORISTS

The theorists have failed to take into account an essential part of man's humanness—his penchant for maddening inconsistency. They hate to force the troubling fact that unlike the phenomena of chemistry or physics—where water always boils at 212 degrees Fahrenheit—humans often behave in unexpected ways (Clemens & Mayer).

Chapter Five
Managing Your Reading and Learning

"Apply thine heart unto instruction, and thine ears to the words of knowledge. Hear thou, my son, and be wise, and guide thine heart in the way. Buy the truth, and sell it not; also wisdom and instruction, and understanding" (Proverbs 23:12, 19).

To paraphrase the great Harvard University teacher and psychologist, William James, "Let not students worry about the success of their efforts. If they will do each day as best they can the work which is before them, they will wake up one day to find themselves among the competent people of their generation." Several years ago the Advertising Council developed a marketing plan to urge young people to read, and their main slogan was "Reading is Fundamental." While this may be true, there are certain guidelines that will perhaps aid you in your quest for knowledge. From her book, *Managing Your Reading*, Phyllis A. Miller suggests the following:

1. Thumb through the book. Look at the print size, and the subheads, the length of the chapters, the graphics.
2. Check the table of contents. It can give you (or fail to do so) a quick view of the author's outline of topics and ideas. Some are more clever than informative, and may hinder your initial entry to the book.
3. Look for other helps. Are there appendices with extra information? Is there a good subject index?
4. Read about the author. This will help you to judge how reliable that person is.
5. Check the copyright date. With the rapid growth of information, books become outdated very quickly. This can alert you to what you may want to reject in the writing.
6. Identify the major points of the book—what is said in a nutshell about the topics or issues addressed in the book.
7. Identify the key concept words—words indicating leading ideas. They may be found in the table of contents.
8. Read a chapter that seems most to capture your attention, or that seems most significant.
9. And now, start on page one.[30]

Miller's example is excellent, but bear in mind these concepts will no doubt only apply to new publications you may wish to examine. The classics, on the other hand, will be approached differently as common sense suggests.

Have you ever noticed the most successful people you have known seem to be great listeners? In fact, you just simply enjoy being around them and feel you could talk to them all day if they would permit? These people have learned one very important aspects in life: learning requires listening more than talking. Also, experience is the accumulated knowledge you yourself have acquired and created in your mind. Imagination allows you to envision what may work in the future and to investigate various alternatives. Reason is the formal rule of thinking you use to bring all of your experiences and imagination to test the accuracy of your beliefs, present and future.

Needless to say, many of us begin this experiment with what is called a "rigid mind." Here, the person insists on simple truths and easy answers, and rejects complexity, doubt, and factual accounts. In short, the rigid mind lacks imagination and insists on the knowledge it already has.

Memory is the basis of all accumulated knowledge and most of us forget about 80 percent of all the information we receive during our lifetime. Take notes and listen; buy packets of legal pads and write down everything you yourself deem important: dates, names, times, events, biographies, authors, books, etc. Unconscious habits can create or destroy your efforts. Conscious repetition of an action over a period of time will make a habit. You cannot change your habits until you become fully aware of them. Take an inventory and make a priority list of your reading and the time you will devote to it each day. Do this week after week and soon your old habits will be replaced with new and more productive ones.

If you search the parks and places where monuments are displayed in the nation, you will not find one statue dedicated to a committee. Your effort will be individual.

YOUR INTUITION IS BETTER THAN YOU THINK

A host of recent research indicates that our intuition is much savvier and more reliable than most corporations would ever admit. Today, institutes from Harvard to the U.S. Marine Corps support research on the power of our subconscious mind. "Many emotions are products of evolutionary wisdom, which probably has more intelligence than all human minds together, " says New York University neural scientist Joseph LeDoux in his book "The Emotional Brain: The Mysterious Underpinnings of Emotional Life." Timothy D. Wilson, professor of psychology at the University of Virginia, conducted a study that revealed that people who choose a poster for their living room wall on gut instinct were much happier with their choice than people who deliberated over the decision. Reporting on this finding and others, Sharon Begley in the "Wall Street Journal" noted, "there is growing consensus that the unconscious is a pretty smart cookie, with cognitive capacities that rival and sometimes surpass that of conscious thought." Picasso claimed that his genius resided in his intuitive self when he said, "Painting is stronger that I am. It makes me do what it wants."

"Women's intuition has been scientifically tested and measured since the late 1980s and, for the most part, comes down to a woman's superiority in all the perspective senses," claims Barbara and Allan Pease in "Why Men Don't Listen and Women Can't Read Maps." David G. Myers, in "Intuition: Its Powers and Perils," seems to agree, stating that there is a "gender gap," that "women generally surpass men at decoding emotional messages." He cites research that says that although boys average 45 points higher on the SAT math tests, however, "girls surpass boys in reading facial expressions."
Is this very important? YES IT IS!

(Source: *BANG! Getting Your Message Heard in a Noisy World* by Linda Kaplan Thaler and Robin Koval, Currency-Doubleday Publishers, 2003. pp-109, 110,113).

Chapter Six
The Success Bookshelf

During my early twenties I began to discover wonderful authors such as Earl Nightengale, Napoleon Hill, William Danforth, Russell Conwell, and practically anything by anyone else I could find if it had to do with self-motivation, leadership, and self-talk to success. My intense pursuit began to intensify following each completed work. With quotes from highly successful people such as Bruce Barton (1886-1967)—founder of one of the most successful advertising agencies in the nation, Batten, Barton, Durstine, and Osborn (BBD&O)—I only became more determined to read and discover their secrets. Barton once said, "In my library there are about a thousand volumes of biography–a rough calculation indicates that more of these deal with men who have talked themselves upward than with all the scientists, writers, saints, and doers combined. Talkers have always ruled. They will continue to rule. The smart thing is to join them."

Over the years I have been assisted by the various books I will share with you, and some I have only looked at in summary. Each one has a message in and of itself; each one will help you greatly in your effort to learn. As Ben Sweetland said, "Success is a journey, not a destination."

The list of various publications in this chapter is far from complete and by no means a definitive master work. It is a place to begin and one I recommend to all of my students. Think of many of these as testimonies, if you will, for what God will do for one, He will do for you. "But wisdom is justified of her children" (Matthew 11:19; see Luke 7:35).

SUGGESTED SUCCESS READING

5 Minutes a Day to Perfect Spelling	by	J. Mark Dufner and Kevin Trudeau
7 Habits of Highly Effective People	by	Stephen R. Covey
101 Ways to Promote Yourself	by	Raleigh Pinskey
A Brief History of Time	by	Stephen Hawking
Accomplishment: The Science and Practice	by	Peter Thompson (video tape)
Assertiveness	by	C. Beels, B. Hopson, M. Scally
Being the Best	by	Denis Waitley
Career Survival	by	Edgar H. Schein
Charisma: Seven Keys to Developing	by	Tony Alessandra

Communication Skills to Inspire	by	Barrie Hopson and Mike Scally
Conversation Power	by	James K. VanFleet (audio tape)
Flirting for Success: The Art of Building Rapport	by	Jill Spiegel
Flow	by	Mihaly Csikszentmihalyi
Four Days With Dr. Deming	by	William J. Latzka and David Saunders
Getting Rich in America	by	Brian Tracy
Goals	by	Zig Ziglar
Happy, Healthy, and Terrific	by	Ed Foreman
Health, Wealth, and Happiness	by	Ed Foreman
High Impact Communication	by	Bert Decker
How to Be a No Limit Person	by	Wayne W. Dyer (video tape)
How to Be a Winner	by	Zig Ziglar (video tape)
How to Gain Power and Influence with People	by	Tony Alessandra
How to Make a Habit of Succeeding	by	Mack R. Douglas and Heartsill Wilson
Infinite Self	by	Stuart Wilde
In the Spotlight: Overcome Your Fear of Public Speaking	by	J. Esposito
In Search of the Invisible Forces	by	George Addair
Intuition	by	Marcia Emery
It's Not What Happens to You, It's What You Do About It	by	W. Mitchell
Lead the Field	by	Earl Nightengale
Leadership Secrets of Attila the Hun	by	Wes Roberts
Leading an Inspired Life	by	Jim Rohn
Life Skills	by	Richard J. Leider
Light Her Fire	by	Ellen Kreidman
Master Strategies for Higher Achievement	by	Brian Tracy
Mind Mapping	by	Michael Gelb
Mission: Success!	by	Og Mandino

Motivation to Excellence	by	Elliot Johnson
NLP:The New Technology of Achievement	by	Hallborn, Smith, et. al
On Becoming a Leader	by	Warren Bennis and Robert Townsend
On Success	by	Earl Nightengale
People Smarts	by	Tony Alessandra
Positive Attitude Training	by	Michael Broder
Protect Yourself	by	Master Tsai
Psychology of Human Motivation	by	Denis Waitley
Psychology of Winning	by	Denis Waitley
Seeds of Greatness	by	Denis Waitley
Sell Your Way to the TOP	by	Zig Ziglar
Shackleton's Way	by	Margot Morrell
Succeed by Listening	by	Madelyn Burley-Allen
Success and the Self Image	by	Zig Ziglar
Success through a Positive Mental Attitude	by	Napoleon Hill and W. Clement Stone
Talking with Confidence for the Painfully Shy	by	Milo O. Frank
Talk Your Way to the Top	by	Kevin Daley
The Art of Exceptional Living	by	Jim Rohn
The Bible		
The Book of Virtues	by	William J. Bennett
The Courage to Live Your Dreams	by	Les Brown
The Dynamics of Effective Listening	by	Tony Alessandra
The Eagle's Secret	by	David McNally
The Genius Formula	by	Tony Bergan and Raymond Keene
The Greatest Secrets of Success	by	Og Mandino (video tape)
The Inner Winner	by	Denis Waitley
The Master of Success	by	Napoleon Hill
The New Dynamics of Goal Setting	by	Denis Waitley
The On-Purpose Person	by	Kevin W. McCarthy
The Power of Ambition	by	Jim Rohn
The Power of Positive Thinking	by	Norman Vincent Peale
The Power of Visualization	by	Lee Pulas

The Psychology of Achievement	by	Brian Tracy
The Psychology of High Self-Esteem	by	Nathaniel Branden
The Psychology of Success	by	Brian Tracy
The Pyramid of Success	by	Jim Harrick and John Wooden
The Science of Personal Achievement	by	Napoleon Hill
The Science of Personal Growth	by	Pat Ryan
The Science of Self-Confidence	by	Brian Tracy
The Strangest Secret	by	Earl Nightengale
The Student Success System	by	Blaine Athorn and Dan Colton
The Successful Communicator	by	Earl Nightengale
There Are No Limits	by	Danny Cox
Think and Grow Rich!	by	Napoleon Hill
Think Big	by	Ben Carson
Thinking: The Human Core	by	Ellen McPeek
TOP Performance	by	Zig Ziglar
Total Self-Help	by	John Ingram Walker
Unlimited Power	by	Anthony Robbins
Vocab	by	Bergen Evans (audio tape)
What Every Young Person Should Know	by	Earl Nightengale
Winning with Words	by	William A. Koehnline

As mentioned earlier, this is by no means a definitive work on all resources available to those who will search them out. Knowledge is free; make use of the public libraries. All great things have a beginning and we have to do everything for the first time. Select a book, video tape, or cassette you feel will help you the most to get started. Take notes and internalize the information you deem worthy to remember for future reference. One helpful method is the three-ring binder. As you make various notes, place them in your binder as references. Memory cannot always be trusted; make written notations as you go. Reading a book without taking notes is simply useless. Obviously, not all can be recalled from memory but writing down important items for a later advantage is worthwhile.

The next list following is not necessarily success and motivational reading but more of the nature of providing a greater insight into learning and observation. This is a foundational list to be added to with other suggested readings throughout this text.

1. George Washington's letter to the Jewish congregation at Newport.
2. Thomas Jefferson: First and Second Inaugurals; Virginia Bill of Religious Liberty; letters to John Adams on Natural Aristocracy; various articles from the Federalist Papers; Constitution of the United States.
3. Certain discussions and statements of John Marshall.
4. James Monroe's promulgation of the Monroe Doctrine.
5. The Constitution of the Anti-Slavery Society.
6. Horace Mann's Twelfth Report to the Massachusetts Board of Education.
7. The Seneca Falls Declaration on Women's Rights.
8. Abraham Lincoln's "House Divided" speech of 1858
9. John Brown's speech to the court that sentenced him.
10. The Declaration of Independence

He who knows not and knows not he knows not,
He is a fool–shun him.
He who knows not and knows he knows not,
He is ignorant–teach him.
He who knows and knows not he knows,
He is asleep–wake him.
He who knows and knows he knows,
He is wise–follow him.
--Arabian Proverb

Without doubt, there is a descending of our great Western culture; and as such, the past is no longer studied as once it was in American colleges and universities. With this thought in mind, the following is offered as a brief, basic overview of what was once valued in American education but is no longer.

CLASSICAL:
Homer
Sophocles
Thucydides
Plato
Aristotle
Vergil

MEDIEVAL:
Dante
Chaucer
Machiavelli
Montaigne
Shakespeare
Hobbes
Milton
Locke

EIGHTEENTH-TWENTIETH CENTURY EUROPE:
Swift
Rousseau
Austen
Wardworth
Tocqueville
George Elliot
Dostoyevsky
Marx
Nietzsche
Tolstoy
Mann
T.S. Eliot

AMERICAN LITERATURE AND HISTORICAL DOCUMENTS:
Declaration of Independence
The Federalist Papers
The Constitution
The Lincoln-Douglas Debates
Lincoln's Gettysburg Address and Second Inaugural Address
Martin Luther King's "Letter from the Birmingham Jail" and "I Have a Dream" Speech

CONFIDENCE

Study after study has shown that those with confidence prevail. Insurance companies that hire thousands of new agents have found that academic records and test scores are not nearly as helpful in predicting which ones will succeed, as is an accurate assessment of a person's tendency to be confident and optimistic.

On the other hand, people who are pessimistic, who lack confidence, tend to fail. Yet, most companies do not train their employees in confidence, or do not devote nearly as much time and efforts to it as they do to teaching something like computer skills. That's because computer skills are tangible and measurable. Confidence happens to be neither.

The good news about confidence is that you get to choose whether you're going to have it. Some people have to work at it harder than others, but confidence is a skill like any other. It can be learned and it must be practiced. Remember, if you want to succeed greatly, you must learn to be confident.[31]

Do All the Good You Can

Do all the good you can,
By all the means you can,
In all the ways you can,
In al the places you can,
At all the times you can,
To all the people you can,
As long as ever you can.
--John Wesley

Chapter Seven
100 Things You Should Know

Wisdom is better than strength: nevertheless the poor man's wisdom is despised, and his words are not heard. The words of wise men are heard in quiet more than the cry of him that rules among fools. Wisdom is better than weapons of war: but one sinner destroys much good (Ecclesiastes 9:18).

Put another way by Percy W. Bridgman, "There are techniques of being intelligent. It is not easy to acquire the proper use of the mental tools that we have thoughtlessly inherited or which are implicit in the construction of our brains. Severe effort and long practice are required."

Yes, reading can be found a task, and remembering what one reads is an even greater challenge. The best advice is to take it slow, go over what is not understood clearly and continue to go over it until it becomes clear. This may require seeking advice from others. Get set for hard work.

Some years ago, I came across an article written by Judy Jones and William Wilson for *Esquire Magazine*. The title of the article was "100 Things Every College Graduate Should Know."

BOOKS TO READ

1.   *The Canterbury Tales*, Geoffrey Chaucer: You'll simply never get all twenty-four tales down pat with Monarch Notes. Purists insist it be taken straight, in original Middle English version.

2.   *Tristram Shandy*, Laurence Sterne: The ultimate book about writing a book and about what goes wrong whenever you try to tell someone else where you're coming from.

3.   *Faust*, Part I, Goethe: A museum piece that refuses to gather dust, with themes to fit just about any occasion: lately, it seems to be about ambition and a man undergoing a mid-life crisis.

4.   *Gulliver's Travels*, Jonathan Swift: Admittedly, it would be more fun if you understood the historical references; but the vocabulary will pop up all your life, and there is no way to understand words like "Brobdingagian" without having been there.

5.   *The Oresteria, Aeschylus*: Greek drama at its most monumental. Cast of characters par excellence: Agamemnon, Clytemnestra, Cassandra, Aegisthus, and the kids. Sophocles, O'Neil, and Sartre borrowed heavily from this trilogy.

6.　*The Brothers Karamazov*, Fyador Dostoyevsky: You really have to read some Dostoyevsky; and unless you're a psychoanalyst, this one's more fun than *Crime and Punishment*.

7.　*The Life of Samuel Johnson, LL.D.*, James Boswell: The greatest biography in the English language and a gold mine of conspicuous erudition. Ability to quote verbatim Boswell quoting Johnson constitutes the basic literacy test of the intellectual elite; what's more, it can get you through any number of sticky situations.

8.　*General Introduction to Psychoanalysis*, Sigmund Freud: Of course, Freud's a cliché, but so is saying Freud's a cliché. Besides, this is valuable consumer information. Read it and weep.

9.　*Ulysses*, James Joyce: Read it alongside Harry Blamires' *The Bloomsday Book*, a reader's guide that will explain what you don't understand (everything).

10.　*Collected Poems of Wallace Stevens*, Wallace Stevens: The stuff of the seventies; how to combine style with intelligence; how to eschew sentimentality without missing out on pain; how to hold down a full time job and be a creative person, too.

PASSAGES OF POETRY WORTH MEMORIZING
(and where they came from)

11.　For I have known them all already, known them all;
Have known the evenings, mornings, afternoons,
I have heard the voices dying without a dying fall
Beneath the music from a farther room.
So how should I presume?
--From the *Love Song of J. Alfred Prufrock*, T.S. Eliot

12.　Our birth is but a sleep and a forgetting;
The soul that rises with us, out life's star,

Hath had elsewhere its setting,
And cometh from afar;
Not in entire forgetfulness,
And not in utter nakedness,
But trailing clouds of glory do we come…
--From *Intimations of Immorality*, William Wordsworth

13. Know then thyself, presume not God to scan;
The proper study of mankind is man.
--From *An Essay on Man*, Alexander Pope

14. Full fathom five thy father lies;
Of his bones are coral made;
Those are pearls that were his eyes;
Nothing of him that doth fade
But doth suffer a sea change
Into something rich and strange.
Sea nymphs hourly ring his knell
Hark! now I hear them –
Dink, dong, bell.
--"A Sea Dirge," from *The Tempest*, William Shakespeare

15. Ah, but a man's reach should exceed his grasp,
Or what's a heaven for?
--From *Andrea del Sarto*, Robert Browning

16. Go and catch a falling star,
Get with child a mandrake root,
Tell me where all past years are,
Or when cleft the devil's foot…
--From "Song," John Donne

17. The world was all before them, where to choose
Their place of rest, and Providence their guide:
They hand in hand, with wand'ring steps and
slow
Through Eden took their solitary way.
--Final lines of *Paradise Lost*, John Milton

18. Is it not passing brave to be a king
"And ride in triumph through Persepolis?"
--From *Tamburlaine the Great*, Christopher Marlowe

19. Bolt the bar and shutter
For the foul winds blow:
Our minds are at their best this night,
And I seem to know
That everything outside us is
Mad as the mist and snow
--From *Mad As the Mist and Snow*, W.B. Yeats

20. Ou sont les neiges d'antan?
--From the *Greater Testament*, Francois Villon

IMPORTANT DISTINCTIONS

21. **Induction vs. deduction**: "Induction" is reasoning from particular cases to general principles, i.e., the scientific method: you look at a number of examples, then come to a general conclusion based on evidence. For instance, having known twenty-five people named Alice, all of whom were women, you might naturally conclude, through induction, that all people named Alice are women. The problem with inductive reasoning, however, is Alice Cooper… is a man. "Deduction" is reasoning from the general to the particular. One starts from a statement, known or merely assumed to be true, and uses it to come to a conclusion about the matter at hand. Once you know that all people have to die sometime and that you are a person, you can logically deduce that you, too, will have to die sometime.

22. **A priori vs. a posteriori**: Adjective phrases describing two kinds of knowledge. "A priori" refers to knowledge that is not dependent on sensory experience of the word (for example, that two plus two equals four) and may be held true with absolute certainty. "A posteriori" knowledge is derived from experience (for example, that objects will fall through space at a given rate) and involves a high degree of probability, not certainty.

23. **Infer vs. imply**: The difference here is simply a matter of where you stand, whether you're on the giving or receiving end. You "imply" something in a remark to a friend who "infers" something from your remark.

24. **Discreet vs. discrete**: "Discreet" is what you should be when you're having an illicit affair. "Discrete," on the other hand, is a learned word meaning separate or detached and has applications in science, medicine,and logic. Example: Matter is made up of discrete units called molecules.

25. **Uninterested vs. disinterested**: You give yourself away when you confuse the two. The former means indifferent; the other means impartial. It's that simple.

26. **Solecism vs. solipsism**: A "solecism" is a particularly unsophisticated blunder in speaking or writing, such as using "ain't" or saying "he and I was." "Solipsism" is a full-blown philosophical theory stating that the self is the only knowable thing, the only reality. By extension, solipsism has come to mean absolute egoism.

27. **Egoist vs. egotist**: Each thinks he is the center of the universe, but the "egoist" could tell you why; he believes that morality is based on self-interest. The "egotist" has never stopped talking about himself long enough to think about it.

28. **Sententious vs. tendentious**: One doesn't want to be either of these. The first suggests affectation or pompous moralizing; the second, the relentless proselytizing of the tract writer.

29. **Pathos vs. bathos**: "Pathos" is the quality in art or literature that stimulates pity or compassion in the onlooker. "Bathos," from the Greek word meaning deep, represents a downward slide into the utterly banal or the unbearably maudlin. Pathos is to bathos as sublime is to the ridiculous. By the way, that's a long "o" in both words.

30. **Sensuous vs. sensual**: Both adjectives refer to the satisfaction of the senses, but "sensuous" usually refers to the kind of pleasure you get from art, music, and the like. "Sensual" has most to do with erotic pleasure. Just remember that whoever wrote *The Sensuous Woman* was confused.

ADJECTIVES YOU HAVE TO LOOK UP EVERY TIME

31. **Noisome**: Harmful, unhealthful, offensive; used especially of a smell.

32. **Fulsome**: Nauseating, repulsive, displaying insincerity, baseness of motive or simple bad taste.

33. **Inchoate**: Just begun, incomplete, imperfectly formulated, incoherent. Pronounced "inko'it."

34. **Jejune**: Insubstantial, insipid, weak. Also, childish or immature.

35. **Lambent**: Flickering lightly over a surface, having a gentle glow. By extension, flitting over subjects with effortless brilliance, as in "a lambent way."

36. **Plangent**: Striking with a deep, reverberating sound, as waves against the shore. Also, plaintive, expressing sadness.

37. **Gnomic**: Aphoristic, expressing a general truth in a few words.

38. **Numinous**: Dedicated to or hallowed by a deity; said especially of places, as in "a numinous wood." Holy, inspiring reverence, appealing to the spirit.

39. **Atavistic**: Reverting to ancestral type.

40. **Protean**: Changing form or essence easily and often; variable, versatile.

IN ANOTHER LANGUAGE
(German)

41. **Weltanschauung**: World view.

42. **Ubermensch**: Nietzche's Superman. Not to be confused with urban mensch.

43. **Doppelganger**: The ghostly double of a living being.

44. **Schadenfreude**: Malicious delight in the bad fortune of others.

45. **Lebensraum**: Literally, room for living. The reason Japan invaded China.

(Latin)

46. **Mutatis mutandis**: Means something like "with the necessary changes or substitutions having been made" or "with the necessary differences having been considered."

47. **Sui generis**: Suggests something so much of its own kind or in a class by itself that "there's no point in analyzing or judging it along established lines."

48. **Ecce homo**: Literally, "Behold the man;" Pilate said it first when he presented Christ, with his crown of thorns, to the mob. "Ecce," even standing alone, has come to be a way of pointing out somebody who's being persecuted unjustly.

49. **Obiter dictum**: Literally, a thing said "by the way," a kind of parenthetical remark. It's not that obiter dictum can't be fascinating, even relevant; they're just never binding.

50. **Sub rosa**: A very fifties phrase. It means covertly, confidentially; derives from Cupid's having given somebody a rose to keep him from publicizing the indiscretion of his mother. You remember–Venus.

LEADEN PRHASES THAT CARRY A LOT OF WEIGHT

51. **Negative capability**: Keat's idea. He defines it as "capable of being in uncertainties, mysteries, doubts, without any irritable reaching after fact and reason." F. Scott Fitzgerald took this idea and gave it a twentieth-century twist, writing, in *The Crack-Up*, (1936), "The test of a first-rate intelligence is the ability to hold two opposed ideas in the mind at the same time and still retain the ability to function. One should, for example, be able to see that things are hopeless and yet be determined to make them otherwise."

52. **Categorical imperative**: Fram Kant. Its basic formulation is: "Act only on that maxim whereby thou canst at the same time will that it should become a universal law." An eighteenth-century German's way of rephrasing the golden rule.

53. **Cognitive dissonance**: Psychological theory evolved in the late Fifties and popular inclusion in introductory psychology courses throughout the Sixties. It's basic premise: We try to transform any bad experience assuming that we've voluntarily chosen it into a good one. Example: "It may not have been a good marriage, but it taught me a lot."

54. **Pathetic fallacy**: Ascribing human passions into nature, John Ruskin cited the classic example: "They rowed her in across the rolling foam – the cruel, crawling foam," and noted snidely, "The foam is not cruel, neither does it crawl." Not a bad thing for a writer to use to show how his characters' minds work when they're upset. If overused, can have a lugubrious effect, as in much of Hardy.

55. **Polymorphous perversity**: The theory that the sex instinct in a child has no predetermined outlet, but leads to various behaviors that would be called perversions in an adult.

FUN WITH NUMBERS

56. **Unit rule**: At former Democratic national conventions, the rule that said a state's entire vote must go to the candidate preferred by the majority of that state's delegates.

Binary system: Mathematical system suggested by Leibnitz in which the base of notation is two instead of ten. Most computers work on the binary system.

Three dramatic unities: (also called the Aristotelian unities) The rules governing the so-called classical drama. They are: (1) unity of action: a logical connection between incidents; (2) unity of time: about twenty-four hours; and (3) unity of place. The unities dominated the theater of seventeenth-century France; you'll find the classic discussion of them in Samuel Johnson's *Preface to Shakespeare.*

Four humors: Medieval theory that the body was composed of sour liquids: blood, phlem, yellow bile, and black bile. They were thought to correspond to the four principal temperaments defining character: the sanguine (cheerful and optimistic), the phlegmatic (not easily aroused), the choleric and the melancholic. The system lacked subtlety but made it a lot easier to pick your friends.

Fifth column: Traitors, enemy sympathizers. A general in the Spanish civil war started this one when he bragged that he had four columns encircling Madrid and a fifth working for him within the city.

Six Characters in Search of an Author: Pirandello's 1921 play in which actors rehearsing a play are interrupted by six people claiming to be characters in it and demanding to add to the play the parts left out by the author.

Things that come in sevens:
Seven Wonders of the Ancient World: The pyramids of Egypt, the

Hanging Gardens of Babylon, the Tomb of Mausalus, the Temple of Diana at Ephesus, the Statue of Zues by Phidas, the Colossus of Rhodes, the Pharos of Alexandria.

Seven Wonders of the Modern World: The Colosseum, the Catacombs of Alexandria, the Great Wall of China, Stonehenge, the Leaning Tower of Pisa, the Porcelain Tower of Nanking, the Mosque of San Sophia at Constantinople.

Seven deadly sins: pride, lust, envy, wrath, avarice (covetousness), gluttony, sloth.

Seven virtues: faith, hope, charity, justice, fortitude, prudence, temperance.

Seven seas: Arctic, Antarctic, Indian, North and South Atlantic, North and South Pacific.

There are also the Seven Hills of Rome and the Seven Ages of Man. These last two can be looked up at your discretion.

TWO HISTORICAL EVENTS WITH ONE WONDERFUL NAME:
THE BABYLONIAN CAPTIVITY

57(58). The first one is no problem because it was a real captivity: It refers to the enslavement of the Jews in Babylon after Nebuchadnezzar's destruction of Jerusalem in 576 BC; just remember Shadrach, Meshach, and Abednego. The second is metaphorical and covers that complex period of medieval history during which the church, already weakened by the emergence of nations-states and the bourgeoisie, decided to trade its integrity for a taste of French cooking. In 1309, papal authority was at such a low ebb that Phillip IV of France was able to dictate the appointment of a Frenchman, Clement V, as pope. Clement promptly returned the favor by moving the papacy from Rome to Avignon, where it remained a tool of the French monarchy until England finally got fed up and forced Pope Gregory XI to move back to Rome in 1377. This second "Babylonian Captivity" irretrievably undermined the credibility of the church throughout the Christian world and led directly to the Great Schism of 1378-1417; it is generally acknowledged that we've never had a more stylish set of popes.

MOVEMENTS BEGINNING WITH THE LETTER "F"

59. **Fabian Society**: Founded in London in 1884 by a group of middle-class intellectuals (including GB Shaw and Sidney Webb) to promote an extremely gentle form of socialism. Its members, who preferred John Stuart Mill to Karl Marx, believed that the existing structure of the state was to be "captured and used," not destroyed, and that "the greatest happiness of the greatest number" could be secured only through that state's stepped-up intervention in economic matters. Instrumental in the founding of Britain's Labour Party in 1906. From Fabius, a Roman general nicknamed "The Delayer," whose tactic of avoiding pitched battles resulted in his eventual victory over stranger forces.

60. **Falangism**: The most important gain achieved by fascism outside of Italy and Germany, the Flangist movement revived the dream of Spain's golden age with its American and Pacific empires. Was founded in 1933 and subsequently joined with such stalwarts of the old order in Spain as monarchists, clericals, and army officers to form the nationalist front in the civil war of 1936-1939. Later adopted by Franco as the state's one official party.

61. **Fauvism**: Modern art at its happiest, characterized by the violent and arbitrary use of color and by an exuberant simplicity. The feeling is one of open windows and healthy metabolisms. Essentially a youth movement, Fauvism lasted only through the century's first decade and brought together such young artists all French as Matisse (its spiritual and actual leader), Derain, Broque, Dufy, Vladminck, Rouault. All later went on to other things. The term "les Fauves," used to refer to painters themselves, means wild beasts and was all one stunned critic could manage when he first saw the artists' work.

62. **Fourierism**: Utopian system, essentially socialist in nature, worked out in crazily graphic detail by Francios Fourier (1772-1837), French economist and reformer. All society was to be organized into phalanxes, each having sixteen hundred people sharing a set of common buildings, and the most menial jobs would pay best. The phalanxes were to be joined to form suitable groups and finally one giant confederation with its capital at Constantinople. Silly, perhaps, but the idea caught on, especially in the United States, where Brook Farm was first a Fourierist showcase, then a Fourierist embarrassment.

63. **La Fronde**: The French civil war of 1648-1652, considered by many historians to be the most costly and least necessary such war. Cardinal Mazarin, successor to Cardinal Richelieu, advisor to the very young Louis XIV and hence the spokesman for the French monarchy, found himself up against a wildly assorted group of nobles, bourgeois, mercenaries, peasants, and Spaniards, all of whom felt they had something to gain from a diminution of royal and ministerial powers. But the fronduers – especially the aristocrats behind the whole thing – could not suppress petty interests long enough to coordinate their efforts, and their revolution, which could have checked the advance of absolute monarchy in France, wound up assuring its preeminence. The word "fronde" means sling and refers to the mob's pelting of Mazarin's window with stones.

64. HOT ROCKS

Black stone: The famous stone kissed by every pilgrim to the Kaaba at Mecca. Muslims say it was white when it fell from heaven but turned black because of the sins of mankind.

Philosopher's stone: The hypothetical substance that, according to the alchemists, would convert all base metals to gold. It motivated so much intense research throughout the Middle Ages that it led, accidentally, to the discovery of the composition of gun powder, the properties of acids, the nature of gas, and the best way to manufacture Dresden porcelain, among other kinds, and cumulatively laid the foundations of the science of chemistry.

Rosetta stone: The stone discovered in 1799 at Fort St. Julien, near Rosetta in the Nile delta, that furnished the key to deciphering Egyptian hieroglyphics. Erected in honor of Ptolemy Epiphanes in 195 BC, it bore an inscription in three languages: the dematic, the hieroglyphic, and the Greek. You can see the Rosetta Stone on display at London's British Museum; and when you're finished, you can pay a visit to the Elgin Marble (Cf. Blarney Stone, stone of Scone, I.F. Stone).

AN AFFAIR TO REMEMBER: THE DREYFUS CASE

65. A national disgrace and a landmark in the history of modern France, this event took place in 1894. Captain Alfred Dreyfus, a Jewish officer in the French artillery, was accused of having betrayed secrets to the Germans. Although the evidence against him was slim, rabid anti-Semitism in the military led a court-martial to convict him of treason and sentence him to life imprisonment on Devil's Island. Two years later new evidence was discovered that pointed to the innocence of Dreyfus and the guilt of an adventurer named Major Esterhazy. But the military authorities, unwilling to admit their error, opted for a cover-up refused to reopen the case. Dreyfus' brother made a few discoveries on his own, however, and soon the case turned into a major political issue with all of France divided into two irreconcilable factions: The Dreyfusards and the anti-Dreyfusards. The former, largely made up of pro-republic, anti-clerical liberals, included Emile Zola, Clemenceau, Anatole France, and other leading intellectuals. Although they were determined to correct the injustice of the affair, the Dreyfusards were less concerned with Dreyfus himself, who was still languishing on Devil's Island, than with discrediting the rightist movement. The anti-Dreyfusards, mostly royalists, militarists, and bigots, felt obliged to resort to perjury and intimidation to protect their idea of patriotism. The plot continued to thicken. Major Esterhazy was tried and acquitted by a court-martial. An outraged Zola wrote his famous open letter

"J'occuse," for which he himself was sentenced to jail. Major Henry, the forger of documents, committed suicide. As Dreyfusards became premier, Dreyfus was retried, convicted again by a military court, then pardoned by the president of France. But pardon, by this time, was not enough; agitation continued in France and throughout the world for his complete exoneration. Finally in 1906, Dreyfus was cleared, and in 1930 his innocence was proven conclusively by the publication of secret German papers. (Esterhazy was, in fact, the culprit.) The repercussions of "l'affaire Dreyfus" were enormous. It completely discredited the monarchist and royalist elements in France and hastened both consolidation of the republic and the separation of church and state. It exposed the extent of corruption in the military and the depth of anti-Semitic feeling throughout the country. The violence of the controversy permeated every level of French society, cutting through friendships and family ties and causing bitter enmity for over a generation. Dreyfus himself, after returning to the army briefly, died in obscurity in Paris in 1935.

IMPORTANT POSSESSIVES

66. **Pascal's wager**: The pragmatic approach to God, and Pascal's attempt to save the skeptical soul through common sense reasoning. Basically, his argument goes: You have everything to gain and nothing to lose by believing in the existence of God. If you win (if God exists), you win everything. If you lose (if God does not exist), you haven't lost a thing.

67. **Occam's razor**: "Entities ought not be multiples, except from necessity." William of Occam's principle of eliminating all unnecessary facts or constituents from a subject being analyzed. The name derives from the way Occam, a fourteenth-century Franciscan scholar, dissected every question as if with a razor. Basically, all he was saying was, "Get to the bottom line."

68. **Hobson's choice**: No choice at all. The origin of this one is a bit peculiar. Thomas Hobson was an eccentric carrier at Cambridge who refused to let customers hire any horses in his stable but the one that

stood nearest the door. It was his idea of ensuring equal justice for all.

69. **Draco's code**: Draco was a seventeenth-century-B.C. Athenian who drew up a code of laws noted for its severity. (Nearly every violation was considered a capital offense.) Hence the adjective "draconian" to describe any very severe code, provision, or policy.

70. **Say's Law**: "Supply creates its own demand." The first statement of economic equilibrium, put forth by the French economist Jean Baptiste Say. The principle on which classical economists based their insistence that a permanent unemployment situation simply could not exist.

SCIENTIFIC PRINCIPLES FOR ENGLISH MAJORS

71. **The second law of thermodynamics**: In every energy transaction, some of the original energy is always changed into heat energy not available for further transformation. In other words, all forms of energy eventually become heat energy and that heat is dissipated into its surroundings. The implication is that in the past the universe had more energy capable of doing work than it has now, and that someday there won't be anything but heat evenly distributed throughout the universe with no one left to enjoy it.

72. **Archimedes' principle**: The "Eureka" business. While stepping into a bathtub, Archimedes discovered that a body dropped into a liquid will displace an amount exactly equal to its own weight. We call this specific gravity.

73. **Doppler effect**: The change in the frequency of a wave (sound or light) that occurs whenever there is a change in the distance between the source and the receiver. Used to measure distances and movements of stars and planets.

74. **Brownian movement**: The zigzag, irregular motion exhibited by minute particles of solid matter when suspended in a fluid. Named for the botanist who established its existence, the phenomenon is

important because it helps substantiate the kinetic molecular theory of matter which states that matter is composed of tiny particles (molecules) that are constantly in motion.

75. **Le Chatelier's principle**: When the conditions of a stable system are altered, the whole system will shift in an attempt to restore the original conditions. This may not be one of the all-time essential scientific principles, but it has a certain ring to it.

THE PTOLEMAIN SYSTEM

76. In the second century AD, Ptolemy, an Alexandria-based Greek, codified all ancient astronomical beliefs and made his momentous pronouncement that the earth was the entire center of the universe, around which the sun, the planets, and the stars all revolved, and that beyond the orbit of the most distant star lay the empyrean, where angels and immortal spirits lived. The Ptolemaic system was rigorously mathematical and highly persuasive. It was accepted by virtually all educated Europeans until Copernicus' treatise on the Revolution of the Heavenly Spheres (published posthumously in 1543) came along and broke the news that the earth was doing the revolving rather than nesting cozily at the center of things, a theory that was soon to be embroidered and enlarged upon by such as Tycho Brahe, Kepler, Galileo, and Newton. Exit angels and immortal spirits. Enter the spirit of doubt.

THE PROPER SEQUENCE OF TAXONOMIC CLASSIFICATION

77. Fauna: (e.g., the Siberian tiger)

Kingdom: Animalia (animals)

Phylum: Chordata (chordates)

Subphylum: Vertebrata (vertebrates)

Class: Mammalia (mammals)

Order: Carnivara (carnivores)

Family: Felidae (cats)

Genus: Panthera (lion, tiger, leopard, jaguar)

Species: Panthera tigris (tiger)

Subspecies: Panthera tigris longpilis (Siberian tiger)

MUSIC (Correct Pronunciations to avoid embarrassment)

78. Pierre Boulez: (boo-lays)

79. Antonin Dvorak: (da-voor-schack)

80. Peer Gynt: (pa-ur gu-nt)

81. Hector Villa-Lobos: (vay-layh loh-boosh)

82. Kurt Vil: (viel)

83. Major theme: Schubert's "Unfinished" Symphony

84. Choral tune: Beethoven's Ninth

85. The Siegried leitmativ: Wagner's Ring of the Nibelung

86. "La ci darem la mano": Mozart's Don Giovanni

87. "Habanera": Bizet's Carmen

88. A compendium of curious facts: 1. A date to remember – May 29, 1913. On this day, "The Rite of Spring" was first performed at the Theatre des Champes-Elysees and provoked one of the most famous

riots in musical history. 2. A Lutheran wrote the greatest Roman Catholic mass of all time (Bach's B-Minor Mass). 3. Mahler wrote ten symphonies, including one not finished and another that he called "Das Lied von der Erde" because he was superstitious and did not want to write more symphonies than Beethoven. 4. Bach's Goldberg Variations were composed for organist and clavierist J.G. Goldberg to use to put a rich man to sleep. Goldberg hung around the hall all night, and whenever the rich man's insomnia persisted, Goldberg played a variation or two. 5. "Le violon d'Ingres" is one of those French expressions for which there is no exact English equivalent. The painter Ingres, it seems, also found time to be quite an accomplished violinist; hence the phrase refers to an avocation at which one excels.

TWELVE SLIDES YOU DIDN'T GET AWAY WITH SLEEPING THROUGH

89. **Doric (c 600 BC), Ionic, and Corinthian (c 450 BC) columns**: Just be aware that Doric is earlier, simpler, and native to Greece. Ionic blew in a century later from Asia Minor (you know, Turkey) and betrays a hint of Eastern sensuousness. Corinthian looks like overgrown Ionic; it had its biggest success much later in Rome.

90. **Gothic cathedral floor plan**: Chances are you didn't have much trouble with flying buttresses and stained-glass windows, but do you know the difference between a nave and a nartbex?

91. **Giotto's The Lamentation (1305-06 – fresco, Arena Chapel, Padua)**: Remember the importance attached to the descending slope. Remember the fuss they made over the three-dimensionality of it all.

92. **Donatello's David (c 1430—32), National Museum, Florence**: The first life-sized statue of a nude since antiquity that is wholly freestanding. Professors still have a difficult time explaining why he wears the rather ornate military boots and a hat.

93. **Van Eyck's Giovanni Arnolfini and His Bride (1434), panel, The National Gallery, London**: "The natural world is made to contain the world of the spirit in such a way that the two actually become one. But the question remains, why is she pregnant on her wedding day?"

94. **Raphael's The School of Athens (1510-11) – fresco, Vatican Palace**: Majestic and classical, the perfect embodiment of the spirit of the High Renaissance and one reason a lot of us dropped the course the first semester.

95. **Rembrandt's Self-Portrait (c 1660) – The Lveagh Bequest, Kenwood, England**: Sure you knew who Rembrandt was, but are you able to appreciate him?

96. **Turner's The Burning of the Houses of Parliament (1834-35) – The Cleveland Museum of Art**: Considered the greatest English painter and a virtuoso of the sublime. Grand effects, spectacular use of color and a predilection for disasters to beat Irwin Allen's.

97. **Monet's Le Dejeuner sue l'Herbe (1863), The Louvre, Paris**: This one began with a scandal and an artistic revolution, not to mention a million T-shirts, postcards, and parodies.

98. **Cezanne's Still Life: Jar, Cup, and Fruit (1877) – Metropolitan Museum of Art, New York**: Up from Impressionism. In his determination to reduce nature to geometry, Cezanne didn't make things easy on himself or anybody else. The question is, how many cones, spheres, and cylinders can you find?

99. **Picasso's Les Demoiselles d'Avignon (1906-07) – The Museum of Modern Art, New York**: The title refers not to the Avignon in France, but to a street in the infamous district of Barcelona; and what's more, there are no ladies.

100. **Le Carbusier's Savove House (1929-30) – Poissy-sur-Seine, France**: Remember the Bauhau, the gang of Germans who, in the Twenties, decided it was time to get behind technology? Le Carbu

spread the same functionalist gospel in France with a series of brilliant, if boxy, houses he like to call "machines a habiter." Later he moved on to other things.

And so, "100 Things Every College Graduate Should Know." The authors were correct in their assessment when stating, "Sure this list is arbitrary, but unless you know everything on it, so was your diploma."[32]

Needless to say, there are countless things all college and university students with a diploma should know, and the best thing to hope and pray for is that all is retained and used in proper application in the future. Remember, what is not memorized cannot be utilized. "Apply thine heart unto instruction, and thine ears to words of knowledge. Buy the truth, and sell it not; also wisdom and instruction, and understanding" (Proverbs 23:12, 13).

History is full of those who, for one reason or another, decided to forsake college and advanced education, but in later years, took it upon themselves to "educate themselves to the best of their ability." Their efforts should be applauded, for today, they are running giant companies with high-volume profit efforts based much on their individual self-taught strategies. The material is available, but motivation can only be provided personally.

REDUNDANCIES AND OXYMORONS:

One of the most important aspects of the English language is one's ability to speak it properly. In today's fast-paced world of communication much is lost in translation. It has become so prevalent that we take improper language as, well, proper. Much of this language abuse comes to us from the media be it the Internet or most notably, from newspapers, radio and television. The following is but a mere smattering of what constitutes proper language these days and is only a "small" sample of what NOT to utilize in one's conversation. Remember we are known for the way we express ourselves therefore, eliminate the following from your vocabulary. In terms of the "oxymorons," such as (jumbo shrimp), some will permeate regardless of our best attempts.

REDUNDANCIES

Sum Total
Most Unique
Foreign Imports
IRA Account
HIV Virus
Plans for the Future
First Priority
Active Participant
Located At
Mutual Agreement
Preboarding
Preexisting Mutual Agreement
Tiny Paper Clip
Past History
Most Unique
Untimely Death
New Innovation
Decide One Way or Another
Look Forward
Old Antique
Completely Surrounded
Jewish Rabbi
Tiny Two-Year-Old
The First Annual
At This Point in Time (Right Now?)
I Thought to Myself
Widow Woman
Noon Luncheon

REDUNDANCIES II

Absolutely essential
Audible to the ear
Bisect in two
Call up on the phone
Christmas Eve evening
Combine together
Completely unanimous
Complete monopoly
Consensus of opinion
Cooperate together
Cover over
Descend down
Each and every one
Entirely eliminated
Extreme prime importance
Final end
First beginnings
Four-cornered square
Important essentials
Individual person
Join together
More better
More older
More paramount
More perfect
Most unique
Rise up
Separate out
Small in size
Sunset in the west
Talented genius
This afternoon at 4 pm
This morning at 8 am
Visible to the eye

OXYMORONS

Exact Estimate
Working Vacation
Limited Obligation
Legal Brief
Jumbo Shrimp
Nondairy Creamer
Act Naturally
Found missing
Resident Alien
Genuine Imitation
Same Difference
Almost Exactly
Alone Together
Silent Scream
Small Crowd
New Classic
Clearly Misunderstood
Plastic Glasses
Terribly Pleased
Definite Maybe
Pretty Ugly

ATTITUDES, OPINIONS, AND BELIEFS

An ***ATTITUDE*** is a general disposition or orientation toward objects, people, and ideas usually accompanied by negative or positive judgments.

An ***OPINION*** is a specific judgment that is emotionally neutral.

A ***BELIEF*** is a thought or idea based on knowledge.

FEEL, THINK, AND BELIEVE

When writing and/or speaking, remember you ***FEEL*** with your hands and by- in- large, with your emotions.

When using the word ***THINK***, you are expressing your *opinion*.

When expressing yourself such, as I ***BELIEVE***, you are in effect saying you are stating a commitment.

When you get what you want in your struggle for self
And the world make you king for a day,
Just go to a mirror and look at yourself
And see what THAT face has to say.
For it isn't your father or mother or spouse
Whose judgment upon you must pass
The person whose verdict counts most
In your life
Is the one staring back from the glass.

Some people might think you're a straight
Shooting chum
And call you a great gal or guy
But the face in the glass says you're only a bum
If you can't look it straight in the eye.
That the one you must please, never mind all the rest
That's the one with you clear to the end.
And you know you have passed your most dangerous test
If the face in glass is your friend.
You may fool the whole world down the
Pathway of years
And get pats on the back as you pass,
But your final reward will be heartache and tears
If you've cheated the face in the glass.

Always remember, the "room for improvement is the largest room in the world." A person can always improve and one of the best ways to begin is vocabulary, simple words. Thomas Mann once said, "Speech is civilization itself." Today, the world is bombarded with slang and simple poor speech and poor communication skills. Our language is beautiful, skillful, intriguing, and profound when spoken well. One must learn to take advantage of the spoken word and incorporate extremely colorful words into common vocabulary. The way one speaks tells more about them than any other activity in life. It makes good sense then to choose words and expressions normally employed by reputable speakers in all areas of the country. This is why a collection entitled "Mini-Dictionary" is included in this work. The best method is to attempt to actually write down word usage in a sentence two or three times. Then speak the sentence until it feels comfortable. Choose words to fit several occasions. There are two speech varieties. Familiar speech is normal conversation, correspondence, platform speech, and so on, and the other is formal speech. Always choose words to fit the occasion and avoid the pitfalls of communications. Everyone can learn to speak with greater confidence, fewer errors, and more genuine communication; best of all, it is the optimum learning experience.

Positiveness

There is little doubt that a positive outlook propels while a negative one imprisons. Many studies have shown this. For example, Martin Seligman, a University of Pennsylvania professor and one of the foremost students of optimism, surveyed representatives of a major life-insurance firm. He found that, among the long-term reps, those who confidently expected a good outcome sold 37 percent more insurance than those with negative attitudes. Similarly, amoung the new hires, the optimists sold 20 percent more. Impressed by Seligman's study, the insurer hired 100 applicants who'd failed the standard industry entrance test but scored high on optimism. Those people sold 10 percent more than the average rep. Further research by Seligman and others has shown that hope is a better predictor of college success than traditional test scores.[33]

6,000,000,000 and counting...

As of 12:02 a.m. Oct. 12, 1999, planet earth reached the 6 billion population number, yet amazingly, the world is getting smaller into what we now call "globalization."

If you were to shrink the world's population to a village of 100 people, the following profile would emerge: [34]There would be 57 Asians, 14 North and South Americans and 8 Africans. Fifty-one would be female, 49 male. Seventy would be non-white; 66 would be non-Christian. Eighty would live in substandard housing. Seventy would not be able to read.

Half would suffer from malnutrition. Seventy-five would have never made a phone call. Fewer than one would be on the Internet, and only one would have a college education. Half the entire village's wealth would be in the hands of six people, and all six would be citizens of the United States.[35]

Chapter Eight

You May Not Be First,
But You May Be Next

This chapter is dedicated to a group of people who despite all odds in many cases, succeeded anyway. Many were not the first to attempt what they accomplished, but as the title proclaims, they were next and thus, became first.

Their stories are but a micro look at the human spirit for, in fact, there are countless deeds being recorded at this very moment by people just like them who for whatever reason refuse to accept their present circumstances. The optimum thing to remember for example is, it's not at all important that Abraham Lincoln was born in a log cabin. The important thing is that he got out of the log cabin!

Remember the story of Sir Edmund Hillary and his conquest of Mount Everest. Hillary was perhaps not the most "talented" mountain climber ever to attempt Everest, he just used more effort than his contemporaries. Those who succeed when the world is telling them to give up know as long as they keep trying they'll never be a failure. Failure is not an event, it is a matter of opinion. Perfection is not the goal, excellence is.

In Rudyard Kipling's *Just So Stories*, he explains in mythical fashion how the camel got its hump. It seems that the camel would not work with the other animals. When asked to help the horses, dogs, and oxen, he would reply with a "Humph!" So the animals complained to a genie who appealed to the camel personally. But the camel kept responding with a huffy "Humph!" until the genie literally gave him a "humph" on his back—allowing him to go longer without water so that he would catch up on his work.

Our habits can become literal characteristics. If we wish to create a pleasing character rather than an unappealing one, we need to closely examine our habits. What begins as an occasional slip quickly becomes a bad habit—and can further escalate into a permanent character flaw.

Do you ever catch yourself letting the quality of your work slide just a bit? Do you tune your ears to gossip more than you used to? Is pride creeping up on you? Is your kindness in shorter supply?

Your habits eventually become your character, so take a lesson from the camel. Eliminate your negative qualities now, or, like the camel, you may carry them for a lifetime. The positive qualities of virtuous living will get you over the hump.[36]

The story has assumed mythic proportions, like the sinking of the Titanic or Robert Falcon Scott's doomed race to the South Pole. Shortly after noon on June 8, 1924, the 38-year-old English schoolmaster and Alpinist George Leigh Mallory, along with a young companion, an Oxford engineering student and oarsman named Andrew "Sandy" Irvine, 22, vanished into the mists surrounding the summit of 29,028-ft Mount Everest, the world's highest mountain, never to be seen or heard from again.

For 75 years, their disappearance has loomed, like Everest itself, as both a challenge and a mystery, made all the more memorable by Mallory's classic retort when asked why he wanted to risk all to climb the far-off mountain: "Because it is there." But did he make it to the top? Or did he falter just short of reaching his goal? In May of 1999 an expedition led by veteran American climber Eric Simonson, retracing Mallory's old route on Everest's Tibetan, or north face, seemed to be tantalizingly close to some definitive answers.

On a rocky, windswept slope some 2,000 feet below the summit, expedition member Conrad Anker spotted "a patch of white"—brighter, he says, than any of the snow or rocks around it. Sprawled face down on the mountainside, with arms outstretched and hands dug into the frozen ground, lay the bleached, mummified remains of a man. It was Mallory, his body almost perfectly preserved in the thin, dry air, a safety rope around his waist, and still partly clad in remnants of his tattered cotton, wool, and tweed climbing clothes, the ragged collars stitched with the markings GL MALLORY. He had apparently tumbled wildly down the slope, tried to arrest his descent with his hands, then died shortly thereafter—"still fighting, still gripping the rock to the end," says climber Jake Norton.

Mallory's leathery skin gleamed so brightly that the climber Dave Hahn likened it to "a Greek or Roman marble statue." Mallory's face was the only part of his body unexposed. He a broken right arm, trauma to his shoulder, and fractures of both leg bones just above the top of his single surviving hobnail boot. Even so, the climbers were awed by the physical specimen before them. "We each noticed the muscular arms of the climber," says Hahn. "After all these years, George Mallory still cut an impressive figure."

Aided by a spring with unusually light snow, the team located him just above the ridge crest where an ice ax—presumed to be Irvine's—was recovered in 1933 and on a shelf where a Chinese climber reporting seeing the remains of an "old English dead" in 1975. When the climbers reached under the body, they found letters from Mallory's family, poignantly close to his heart, as well as a broken altimeter, a pocket knife, monogrammed handkerchiefs and other personal items. Intriguingly, a pair of sun goggles found in a pocket suggest that he was trying to descend in fading light. There was, however, no sign of Irvine. With the Mallory family's permission, the team took a snippet of tissue from the forearm in order to compare any surviving DNA with samples from his descendants, including perhaps his grandson George, who reached the summit in 1995. Then they covered the body with rocks and read the Anglican service of committal before descending 10,000 feet for a few days' rest at their base camp.

The expedition, which was filmed by a joint Nova/BBC crew and was posting communiqués on two websites, continued searching in the few remaining weeks of Everest's busy spring climbing season. Besides Irvine's remains, the expedition is eager to find a Kodak vest-pocket folding camera given to Mallory just before the ascent. If he and his young partner made it to the summit, they would undoubtedly have photographed themselves at the top of the world—and those images would probably still be retrievable from film kept in so deep a freeze even after three-quarters of a century.

Meanwhile, the arguments continue to rage over whether Mallory and Irvine made it all the way, beating New Zealander Edmund Hillary and Sherpa Tenzing Norgay by 29 years. "It's an interesting, romantic thought, but until someone shows a clear image of them at the summit, I'm happy to stick with Hillary and Tenzing," says veteran climber David Breashears. As for the 79-year-old Sir Edmund, he isn't losing any sleep over the matter. "Getting to the bottom is an important part, too," he told Television New Zealand.

The climbers, although initially skeptical, have changed their mind about Mallory. "Just seeing his strength and his obvious tenacity," says Norton, convinces him that Mallory and Irvine "both made it and met their demise on their way down." Still, just as the discovery of the Titanic's fragmented hull stripped that timeless tragedy of some of its fascination, so the sight of Mallory's mortal remains somehow makes this larger-than-life figure more human—and more vulnerable.[37]

Sir Edmund Hillary:

Born July 20, 1919 in Auckland, New Zealand. Mountain climber and Antarctic explorer who, with the Nepalese mountaineer Tenzing Norgay, was the first to reach the summit of Mount Everest, at 29,028 feet, the highest mountain in the world.

A beekeeper by occupation, Hillary began climbing in the New Zealand Alps. In 1951, he joined a New Zealand party to the central Himalayas and then went on to help in a reconnaissance of the southern flank of Everest. In 1953, as a member of the British Everest expedition, he reached the top on May 29 and was knighted for this feat on July 16. He described his exploits in *High Adventure* (1955). Hillary made other expeditions in the Everest region during the early 1960s and built schools, hospitals, and airfields for the Sherpa people who lived there.

Between 1955 and 1958, Hillary commanded the New Zealand group participating in the British Commonwealth Trans-Antarctic Expedition led by Vivian Fuchs. He reached the South Pole by tractor on January 4, 1958, and recorded this feat in *The Crossing of Antarctica* (1958; with Fuchs) and *No Latitude for Error* (1961). On his Antarctic expedition of 1967, Mount Herschel (10,941 feet) was scaled for the first time. In 1977 he led the first jet boat expedition up the Ganges River and continued by climbing to its source in the Himalayas. His autobiography, *Nothing Venture, Nothing Win*, was published in 1975 (from Britannica.com. 1999).

- Mount Everest is the tallest point on earth, standing at 29,028 feet tall.
- It is 5.5 miles above sea level.
- Mount Everest is located half in Nepal and half in Tibet.
- Mount Everest is named for Sir George Everest, the British surveyor-general of India.
- The Tibetan name for Everest is Chomolungma.
- The Nepalese call the mountain Sargarmantha.
- On May 29, 1953, the mountain was first summited by members of a British team.
- Sir Edmund Hillary and Tenzing Norgay, a sherpa, were the first to the top.
- In 1963, the first American, James Whittaker, made the climb.
- Reinhold Messner of Italy and Peter Habler of Austria both scaled Everest without oxygen.
- Wanda Rutkiewicz was the first woman to summit without using oxygen.
- Dick Bass, age 55, became the oldest person to climb Everest.
- The youngest person to ascend Everest was a 17-year-old French student.

Benjamin Carson:

In the fifth grade, Carson was considered the "dummy" of his class. His classmates and teacher took for granted the fact that he took an entire quiz without getting a single question right. His temper was so violent that he would attack other children and even his own mother at the slightest provocation. But Carson turned his life around. He graduated from Yale in 1973 and married Lacena Rustin in 1975. Graduating from Medical School at Michigan, Carson received Magna Cum Laude Award from the American Radiological Society.

Carson made medical history in 1987 with an operation separating Siamese twins. The Binder twins were joined at the back of the head and previous operations to separate twins joined in this way had always failed. A seventy-member surgical team and 22 hours successfully separated the two and they now survive independent of one another.

Carson's other surgical innovations have included the first intrauterine procedure to relieve pressure on the brain of a hydrocephalic fetal twin, and a hemispherectomy, in which an infant suffering from uncontrollable seizures has half of its brain removed. This stops the seizing and the remaining half of the brain actually compensates for the missing hemisphere.

In addition to his surgical duties, Carson addresses junior high and high school students visiting his hospital. His two books, *Gifted Hands* and *Think Big* have inspired readers. The letters in *Think Big* stand for the following:

Talent: Our Creator has endowed all of us not just with the ability to sing, dance, or throw a ball, but with intellectual talent. Start getting in touch with that part of you that is intellectual and develop that, and think of careers that will allow you to use that.

Honesty: If you lead a clean and honest life, you don't put skeletons in the closet. If you put skeletons in the closet, they definitely will come back just when you don't want to see them and ruin life.

Insight: It comes from people who have already gone where you are trying to go. Learn from their triumphs and their mistakes.

Nice: If you are nice to people, once they get over the suspicion of why you're being nice, they will be nice to you.

Knowledge: It makes you into a more valuable person. The more knowledge you have, the more people need you. It's an interesting phenomenon, but when people need you, they pay you, so you'll be okay in life.

Books: They are the mechanism for obtaining knowledge, as opposed to television.

In-depth Learning: Learn for the sake of knowledge and understanding, rather than for the sake of impressing people or taking a test.

God: Never get too big for Him.

Florence Chadwick:

Florence Chadwick was born to the water. At the age of ten, following six years of swimming defeats, she won spectacularly. Chadwick competed against senior swimmers in a two-and-a-half mile night "rough water swim," finishing fourth. At eleven, she won her first race in a six-mile rough water swim in San Diego. Chadwick continued to swim competitively for nineteen years throughout the US.

Turning professional in 1945, Chadwick joined her former teammate, Esther Williams, and appeared in the movie *Bathing Beauty*. 1948 found her training to swim the English Channel. Two years later she would become the first woman to swim that body of water both ways.

While working in San Diego as a stockbroker, she was the only woman on the Board of the San Diego "Hall of Champions." Her devotion to youth groups and encouragement to young people to fulfill their dreams heralds her as a true champion (from www.wic.org/bio/chadwick.htm, 1999).

Max Cleland:

A native Georgian born in 1942, Max Cleland graduated from Lithonia High School in 1960 and was named "Outstanding Senior" in his class by *The Atlanta Journal*. He attended Stetson University where he earned a Bachelor of Arts and took a second lieutenant's commission in the US Army through its ROTC program. He earned his Masters in American History from Emory University. Both schools have since awarded Cleland Honorary Doctorate Degrees.

Cleland volunteered for duty in Vietnam in 1967, where he was promoted to captain in the US Army. After being seriously wounded in a grenade explosion, losing both of his legs and his right arm, Cleland returned to the United States just one month prior to the end of his tour of duty. Since then, he has been awarded the Bronze Star for Meritorious Service and Silver Star for Gallantry in Action.

Cleland served both nation and state for over a quarter of a century. After returning from Vietnam, he was elected to the State Senate in Georgia and as the only Vietnam veteran, he wrote the state law that makes public facilities accessible to the elderly and handicapped.

In 1977, Cleland was appointed by President Jimmy Carter to head the US Veterans Administration. As the youngest ever VA administrator and the first veteran of Vietnam to head the agency, he managed the nation's largest educational assistance program, the VA Home Loan Guaranty program, and administered the largest health care system in the country, the VA Hospital program.

Georgia elected Cleland Secretary of State in 1982, the youngest in the history of the state. There Cleland fought for tougher campaign finance laws and cracked down on securities and telemarketing fraud. In 1995, he implemented the National Voter Registration Act in Georgia, which added almost one million new voters.

Cleland created the First Stop Business Information Center in the Secretary of State's office after conducting public hearings on small business issues throughout Georgia. He won a national award from the US Small Business Administration for his creation of the Center. The Center serves as a one-stop shop for small business owners and entrepreneurs.

In 1996, Cleland was named one of *Time* magazine's Rising Democrats. Jimmy Carter, former President said, Max Cleland is ". . .a strong and forceful leader." The *London Times* said Cleland is ". . .rapidly becoming America's most extraordinary politician." Columnist David Broder of *The Washington Post* has written that Max Cleland ". . .the genuine article. He is an authentic American hero, an inspiration to people everywhere; a living, breathing testament to the power of the human spirit."

Following his service in Vietnam and making his way to recovery, Cleland turned to public service in search of meaning in his life. He often comments that he turned his "scars into stars." Cleland's autobiography title, *Strong at the Broken Places*, comes from a quote by Earnest Hemingway: *"The world breaks everyone and afterward many are strong at broken places."* That describes Cleland and his philosophy – public service is his purpose, and his source of strength. Max Cleland is living proof that obstacles can be conquered (from www.senate.gov/~cleland/biography.htm).

Russell Herman Conwell:

Born February 15, 1843, Conwell was an American lawyer, author, clergyman, and educator whose lecture "Acres of Diamonds," which expressed his formula for success, brought him fame and wealth on the Chautauqua circuit.

In 1862 Conwell began law study at Yale but left a few weeks later to raise a company for service in the American Civil War, in which he was awarded the rank of captain. Admitted to the bar in 1865 (after graduating from Albany Law School, Albany, NY), he practiced law in Minneapolis and Boston. In

1867 he was editor in chief of the *Minneapolis Daily Chronicle*, and he was co-owner of the *Sommerville* (Massachusetts) *Journal.*

Conwell was ordained a minister in 1881 and in 1882 was called to Grace Baptist Church in Philadelphia, a small congregation struggling with debt. The church prospered under his leadership, moving eventually to the much larger Baptist Temple. Conwell founded Temple University in 1884 as a series of night study courses for ministerial students; the school received a college charter in 1888 and became a university in 1907, with Conwell as its first president.

Conwell delivered his lecture "Acres of Diamonds" no fewer than 6,000 times. The theme of the lecture was that opportunity lurks in everyone's backyard. Everyone, Conwell, believed, can and ought to get rich and then use his money for the good of others. "Keep clean, fight hard, pick your openings judiciously, and have your eyes forever fixed on the heights toward which you are headed," was his simple formula for success and the central emphasis of his preaching (from britannica.com, 1999).

Carmen Cozza:
Most famous for his football coaching at Yale University, Cozza accumulated 177 wins throughout 31 seasons. Cozza's strong character and successful tenure will long be remembered following his retirement in 1996. In 1995, he received the George C. Carens Award for the New England Football Writers Association for outstanding contribution to New England football. In 1992, the Walter Camp Football Foundation honored the Ohio native with its Distinguished American Award. The Elis last took the Ancient Eight crown in 1989, the same year Cozza was named Kodak District Coach of the Year in Division I-AA for the seventh time. His many wins, ten Ivy League titles, 18 winning seasons, and six Bushnell Cup recipients are just a few of the countless reasons that he has received so much recognition.

Cozza was born in 1930 in Parma, Ohio. In high school, he earned 11 varsity letters in football, basketball, track, and baseball. He also served as class president his last three years at Parma High and was later inducted into the school's Hall of Fame.

Cozza attended Miami of Ohio and earned six varsity letters, three each in baseball and football. On the field, he played quarterback, running back, and defensive back. He was named to the Miami Hall of Fame, and went on to play professionally for the Cleveland Indians and Chicago White Sox, earning a batting average of .388.

He coached high school football in Ohio and returned to Miami as head freshman football coach in 1956. He was promoted to varsity staff and served there two yeas until leaving to join Yale's squad as a backfield coach. Cozza became head coach in 1965, replacing the resigning John Pont as Yale's 32nd head football coach. The rest is history.

William Edward Burghardt Du Bois:
American sociologist, the most important black protestant leader in the United States during the first half of the 20th century. Born February 23, 1868, he shared in the creation of the National Association for the Advancement of Colored People (NAACP) in 1909 and edited *The Crisis*, its magazine, from 1910 to 1934. Late in life he became identified with Communist causes.

Du Bois graduated from Fisk University, a black institution in Nashville, Tennessee in 1888. He received a Ph.D. from Harvard in 1895. His doctoral dissertation, *The Suppression of the African Slave-Trade to the United States of America, 1638-1870*, was published in 1896. Although Du Bois took an advanced degree in history, he was broadly trained in the social sciences; and at a time when sociologists were theorizing about race relations, he was conducting empirical inquiries into the condition of blacks. For more than a decade he devoted himself to sociological investigations of blacks in America, producing 16 research monographs published between 1897 and 1914 at Atlanta University, where he was a professor, as well as *The Philadelphia Negro: A Social Study* (1899), the first case study of a black community in the United States.

Although Du Bois had originally believed that social science could provide the knowledge to solve the race problem, he gradually came to the conclusion that in a climate of virulent racism, expressed in such evils as lynching, peonage, disfranchisement, Jim Crow segregation laws, and race riots, social change could be accomplished only through agitation and protest. In this view, he clashed with the most influential black leader of the period, Booker T. Washington, who preaching a philosophy of accommodation, urged blacks to accept discrimination for the time being and elevate themselves through hard work and economic gain, thus winning the respect of whites. In 1903, in his famous book, *The Souls of Black Folk*, Du Bois charged that Washington's strategy, rather than freeing the black man from oppression, would serve only to perpetuate it. This attack crystallized the opposition to Booker T. Washington among many black intellectuals, polarizing the leaders of the black community into two wings—the "conservative" supporters of Washington and his "radical" critics.

Two years later, in 1905, Du Bois took the lead in founding the Niagara Movement, which was dedicated chiefly to attacking the platform of Booker T. Washington. The small organization, which met annually until 1909, was seriously weakened by internal squabbles and Washington's opposition. But it was significant as an ideological forerunner and direct inspiration for the interracial NAACP, founded in 1909. Du Bois played a prominent part in the creation of the NAACP and became the association's director of research and editor of its magazine, *The Crisis*. In this role he wielded an unequaled influence among the middle-class blacks and progressive whites as the propagandist for the black protest from 1910 until 1934 (from britannica.com, 1999).

Edward Everett:
Born April 11, 1794, Everett was an American statesman and orator who is mainly remembered for delivering the keynote speech immediately preceding President Abraham Lincoln's Gettysburg Address on November 19, 1863 at the ceremony dedicating the Gettysburg National Cemetery during the American Civil War. The story goes that Abraham Lincoln was invited as an afterthought, and was asked by the organizers to conclude the ceremonies with "a few appropriate remarks." Everett was invited because he was probably the most noted orator of the day. He spoke first and delivered a 2-hour oration, followed by thunderous applause. Lincoln delivered his 4-minute address and sat back down while the crowd stood in dead silence. Disappointed, Lincoln turned to his bodyguard and questioned the lack of response. Everett however, expressed the true feelings of everyone there by declaring to Lincoln that he had said in a few minutes what had taken he, Everett, two hours to capture.

By 1820, Everett had established a formidable reputation as a lecturer and orator, based on careful preparation, an extraordinary memory, and brilliance of style and delivery. He served in the US House of Representatives (1835-39), and as US minister to England (1841-45). With his election as president of Harvard in 1846, he withdrew from politics for several years, returning in 1852 as secretary of state during the last four months of President Millard Fillmore's administration. In 1853 he entered the US Senate, but his generally conciliatory stand on the issue of slavery aroused the ire of his abolitionist constituents, and he resigned the following year.

In 1860 Everett was the unsuccessful vice presidential candidate of the

Constitutional Union Party, which sought to bridge sectional differences by stressing common devotion to the Union and the Constitution. His desire for compromise ended at the outbreak of the Civil War, throughout which he traveled and spoke in support of the Union cause. Everett died on January 15, 1865 (from britannica.com, 1999).

Carleton S. Fiorina:

Carly Fiorina, 45, is president and chief executive officer of Hewlett-Packard Company. HP is a leading global provider of computing, Internet and intranet solutions, services, and communications products, all of which are recognized for excellence in quality and support. The company's headquarters are located in Palo Alto, California.

Fiorina is focused on leading Hewlett-Packard to achieve improved growth in revenue and profitability; greater innovation and inventiveness; the best total customer experience; and on making HP the company that makes the Internet work for customers.

Prior to joining HP, Fiorina spent a total of nearly 20 years at AT&T and Lucent. During the last two years, as president of Lucent's Global Service Provider Business, the division dramatically increased its growth rate, rapidly expanded its international revenues, and gained market share in every region across every product line. In addition, she spearheaded the planning and execution of Lucent's 1996 initial public offering and subsequent spin-off from AT&T, one of the largest and most successful IPO's ever. Prior to Lucent, Fiorina held a number of senior positions at AT&T. She began her career with the company as an account executive.

Fiorina became president and CEO of Hewlett-Packard in 1999, succeeding Lewis E. Platt, who previously had announced his intention to retire. On July 23, 1999, Fiorina was elected to the company's board of directors.

Fiorina holds a bachelor's degree in medieval history and philosophy from Stanford University; a master's degree in business administration from the Robert H. Smith School of Business at the University of Maryland at College Park, Md.; and a master of science degree from MIT's Sloan School.

Fiorina is a member of the boards of directors of the Kellogg Company, Merck & Co. Inc, the US China Board of Trade, and PowerUp, a coalition of business, non-profits, and government to give underserved children access to technology and guidance on how to use technology.

Previously, she held positions on the boards of directors of the USA

Republic of China Economic Council; Goldstar Information & Communications, Inc. of Seoul, Korea; and AT&T Taiwan Telecommunications of Taipei. She also served on the board of the Telecommunications Industry Association.

For the second year in a row, Fiorina topped Fortune magazine's list of the most powerful women in American business.(From Hewlett-Packard Company, 1994-1999, www.hp.com/abouthp/newsroom/bios/fiorina.html).

The reason for Fiorina's success is her independence. Her father always urged his three children to speak their minds; he was a serious and intellectual law professor. Fiorina's mother taught her the power of attitude, she recounted. Fiorina once dreamed of being a classical pianist. She settled eventually on her father's field: law. Her first year she dropped out. At 25, she joined AT&T and worked her way up (*Fortune* magazine, author Patricia Sellers).

Robert Maynard Hutchins:

American educator and university and foundation president, Robert M. Hutchins was born January 17, 1899. Critical of over-specialization, Hutchins sought to balance the college curriculum and maintain the Western intellectual tradition.

Attending Oberlin College in Ohio (1915-17), he served in the ambulance service of the U.S. and Italian armies during World War I. He graduated from Yale University and Law School and was there named dean in 1927. Two years later—aged 30—Hutchins became president of the University of Chicago; there he remained until 1951, the final six years as chancellor. A controversial administrator, he attempted to reorganize the departments for undergraduate and graduate study at Chicago. His Chicago Plan for undergraduates encouraged liberal education at earlier ages and measured achievement by comprehensive examination, rather than by classroom time accumulated. Hutchins argued about the purposes of higher education, deploring undue emphasis on nonacademic pursuits, such as intercollegiate football, and criticizing the tendency toward specialization and vocationalism. The university abandoned the majority of his reforms after his departure, however and returned to its former educational practices, similar to those of other major American universities.

Hutchins played a predominant role in forming the Committee to Frame a World Constitution in 1945, and led the Commission on Freedom of the Press, as well as vigorously defending academic freedom, opposed to faculty loyalty oaths common in the 1950s. Following his service as associate director of the Ford Foundation, Hutchins became president of the Fund for the Republic (1954) and in 1959 founded the Center for the Study of Democratic Institutions as the fund's main activity. The formation of the Center was an attempt to approach Hutchin's ideal of "a community of scholars" discussing a wide range of issues—individual freedom, international order, ecological imperatives, the rights of minorities and women, and the nature of the good life, among other topics.

From 1943 until his retirement in 1974, Hutchins was the chairman of the Board of Editors of *Encyclopedia Britannica* and a director for the same corporation. He also served as editor for various works. His views on education and public issues appeared in a variety of books. Hutchins died May 17, 1977 (from britannica.com, 1999).

Abraham Lincoln:

Born on a Sunday in 1809 in a log cabin near Hodgenville, Kentucky, Abraham Lincoln grew up in a Baptist church that had broken off from another congregation due to the opposing views of slavery. At seven, the family moved to Indiana, where Lincoln attended school and experienced the hardship of his mother's death. He loved learning and preferred reading to working in the fields. His father held the opposite view and this made for a rough relationship between the two. Lincoln was found constantly borrowing books from neighbors.

In 1828, Lincoln's sister, Sarah, died during childbirth. That same year he visited New Orleans and two years later moved west to Illinois. There he worked several jobs, from operating a store to surveying to serving as postmaster. The locals were impressed with Lincoln's character and he gradually earned the nickname "Honest Abe." Lincoln stood nearly 6'4" and served in the Black Hawk War. Soon after he made a run for office in the Illinois legislature and lost. The next four terms he ran again and successfully won. A member of the Whig Party until 1856, Lincoln became a Republican and began to study law.

In 1842, Lincoln married Mary Todd and had four children in the following years. He became a successful attorney and bought a home for his family in Springfield.

Lincoln ran for United States House of Representatives in 1846 and won. He quickly became known in Washington for his opposition to the Mexican War and to slavery. At the end of his term he returned to Illinois and pursued law more passionately than ever.

With the passing of the Kansas-Nebraska Act in 1854, Lincoln's interest in politics dwindled. He unsuccessfully ran for Senate and received support for Vice-Presidential nomination in 1856. Opposed to the Dred Scott decision, Lincoln gave his Lost Speech and "House Divided" Speech surrounding that controversy. He participated in a series of debates with Stephen Douglas, citing his opposition to slavery and its allowance in new territories. Even though Douglas won the Senate race, Lincoln gained national attention.

William Seward was the favored candidate for the Republican Presidential nomination in 1860, but Lincoln won on the third ballot. Elected as the 16th President of the United States, he and his running mate Hannibal Hamlin took office in 1861, defeating Douglas, John Bell, and John C. Breckinridge.

After the election, most Southern states feared Republican control in the government and seceded from the Union. Lincoln faced the greatest internal crisis of any President up to that point. After the defeat of Fort Sumter, Lincoln raised an army and decided to fight for the preservation of the Union. Despite enormous pressures, lost lives, setbacks on the battlefield, generals unprepared to battle, and threats of assassination, Lincoln held firm to his pro-Union policy for four years of Civil War. The Emancipation Proclamation went into effect on January 1, 1863. Lincoln's declaration for the freedom of all slaves in areas of the Confederacy not under Union control led to the famous Gettysburg Address later that year. The battlefield was dedicated to the many Americans who gave their lives for their nation. Lincoln called upon those remaining to finish the work of their predecessors.

In 1864, Lincoln was re-elected as President with running mate Andrew Johnson. The South was slowly being worn down and on April 9, 1865, General Robert E. Lee surrendered to General Ulysses S. Grant. Two days later, Lincoln addressed a crowd outside the White House about the turn of events. Among other things, he suggested he would support voting rights for certain blacks. This infuriated a racist and Southern sympathizer in the audience: John Wilkes Booth hated everything Lincoln stood for.

The Lincoln's attended a play on April 14, 1865 at Ford's Theater. During the performance, Booth arrived at the theater, entered the State Box from the back and shot Lincoln in the head. Lincoln passed away the next morning, the first president ever assassinated in American history. The nation mourned. Lincoln's body was taken to Springfield, Illinois, by train and buried in the

Lincoln Tomb on May 4, 1865. The Reconstruction program took place in America without the man who conceived it.

Lincoln is remembered for his vital role as the leader of preserving the Union during the Civil War and beginning the process leading to the eventual end of slavery in the nation. His character, speeches and letters, and humble beginnings of perseverance and determination make him one of the most famous men of American history (From Abraham Lincoln's Research Site, February 28, 1998).

Nelson Mandela:

Born July 18, 1918 to Chief Henry Mandela of the Xhosa-speaking Tembu tribe, Nelson Mandela was educated at University College of Fort Hare and the University of Witwatersrand and qualified in law in 1942. He joined the African National Congress (ANC) of South Africa in 1944 and five years later became one of that black-liberation group's leaders, assisting to revitalize the organization and engaging in increasingly militant resistance against the apartheid policies of the ruling National Party. Mandela stood trial for treason in 1956-61 but was acquitted. During this time he divorced his first wife and married Winnie Mandela; they divorced in 1996. After the massacre of unarmed Africans by police forces at Sharpeville in 1960 and the subsequent ban of the ANC, Mandela abandoned his nonviolent stance and began to advocate the use of sabotage against the ruling regime of the nation. In 1962, he was again jailed and sentenced to five years' imprisonment.

In 1963, Mandela and other men were all tried for sabotage, treason, and violent conspiracy in the celebrated Rivonia Trial. It was named so for a fashionable suburb of Johannesburg where raiding police had discovered quantities of arms and equipment at the headquarters of the underground Umkhonto We Sizwe ("Spear of the Nation," the ANC's military wing). Mandela had been a founder of the organization and admitted the truth of some of the charges that were made against him. On June 11, 1964, he was sentenced to life imprisonment.

From 1964-82, he was incarcerated at Robben Island Prison, off the coast of Cape Town. He was subsequently kept at the maximum-security Pollsmoor Prison until 1988, at which time he was hospitalized for tuberculosis. Mandela retained wide support among South Africa's black population, and his imprisonment became a cause celebre among the international community that disapproved of apartheid. The South African government under President FW deKlerk released Mandela from prison on

February 11, 1990. On March 2, Mandela was chosen as deputy president of the ANC and he replaced Oliver Tambo as president in 1991.

In 1993, Mandela and deKlerk were awarded the Nobel Prize for Peace for their efforts to end apartheid and bring about a peaceful transition to nonracial democracy in South Africa. Mandela was elected president of the nation in 1994 in the country's first all-race elections. He introduced housing, education, and economic development initiatives designed to improved the living standards of the country's black population (from britannica.com, 1999).

Mother Teresa:

The daughter of an Albanian grocer, Mother Teresa was born in 1910 in Skopje as Agnes Gonxha Bojaxhiu. She went to Ireland in 1928 to join the Institute of the Blessed Virgin Mary, sailing only six weeks later to India as a teacher. She later requested to work with the poor of Calcutta.

After studying nursing, Mother Teresa moved into the slums. Municipal authorities, upon her petition, gave her the pilgrim hostel near the sacred Kali's temple, where she founded her order in 1948. Sympathetic workers soon flooded in to her aid. Dispensaries and outdoor schools were organized. Mother Teresa became an Indian citizen and her fellow Indian nuns all donned the sari as their traditional dress. Mother Teresa's order received canonical sanction in 1950 from Pope Pius XII, and became a pontifical congregation in 1965. The order opened several centers for the blind, aging, crippled, lepers, and dying. Under the guidance of Mother Teresa, the Missionaries of Charity built a leper colony near Asanol, India, called Shanti Nagar (Town of Peace). Mother Teresa continued as the leader of the order, in spite of years of health complications.

The government of India awarded Mother Teresa the "Lord of the Lotus" or Padmashri for her aid to the peoples of India. Pope Paul VI donated his limousine to her when he visited India in 1964 and she immediately raffled it off for aid for the leper colony. Mother Teresa was summoned to Rome in 1968 to build a home there, staffed with Indian nuns. Her missionary work was awarded with the Nobel Prize in 1979.

The Missionaries of Charity number over a thousand. They function out of 60 centers in Calcutta and over 200 centers internationally, including Sri Lanka, Tanzania, Jordan, Venezucla, Great Britain, and Australia (From britannica.com, 1999-2000).

John Reed:
United States poet-adventurer, born October 22, 1887, whose short life as a revolutionary writer and activist made him the hero of a generation of radical intellectuals.

Reed, a member of a wealthy Portland family, graduated from Harvard in 1910 and began writing for a Socialist newspaper, *The Masses*, in 1913. In 1914 he covered the revolutionary fighting in Mexico and recorded his impressions in *Insurgent Mexico* (1914). Frequently arrested for organizing and defending strikes, he rapidly became established as a radical leader and helped form the Communist Party in the United States.

He covered World War I for *Metropolitan* magazine; out of this experience came *The War in Eastern Europe* (1916). He became a close friend of Lenin and was an eyewitness to the 1917 Bolshevik Revolution in Russia, recording this event in his best known book, *Ten Days That Shook the World* (1919).

When the US Communist Party and the Communist Labor Party split in 1919, Reed became the leader of the latter. Indicted for treason, he escaped to the Soviet Union and died of typhus; he was subsequently buried with other Bolshevik heroes beside the Kremlin wall. Following his death the Communist Party formed many John Reed clubs, associations of writers and artists, in US cities. Reed died October 19, 1920 and is the only American buried in Red Square (from britannica.com, 1999).

Paul Robeson:
The son of a former slave turned preacher, Robeson attended Rutgers University in New Brunswick, NJ, where he was an All-American football player. Upon graduating from there at the head of his class, he turned down a career as a professional athlete and entered Columbia University. Obtaining a law degree, he began to pursue a career, but with little opportunity in the 1920s for blacks in the legal profession, he drifted toward acting. Robeson made a London debut in 1992. He joined the Provincetown Players, a New York theatre group that included playwright Eugene O'Neill, and appeared in O'Neill's play *All God's Chillun Got Wings* in 1924. His subsequent appearance in O'Neill's title role in *The Emperor Jones* created a sensation in New York City and London. Robeson also starred in the film version of the play, and pursued the talent he had for singing with his bass-baritone voice. He gave his first vocal recital of Negro spirituals in 1925 in Greenwich Village and became world-famous as Joe in *Show Boat*, singing a rendition of

"Ol' Man River." His characterization of the title role in *Othello* in London won high praise, as did the Broadway production in 1943, setting an all-time record run for a Shakespearean play on Broadway.

Increasing political awareness compelled Robeson to visit the Soviet Union in 1934, and from that year he became increasingly identified with strong left-wing commitments, still pursuing acting and singing, finding success in concerts, recordings, and theatre. In 1950 the US State Department withdrew Robeson's passport as he refused to sign an affidavit disclaiming membership in the Communist Party. In the following years he was virtually ostracized for his political views, although in 1958 the Supreme Court overturned the affidavit ruling. Robeson then left the US to live in Europe and travel in Soviet bloc countries. Because of ill health, Robeson returned to the United States in 1963. He passed away on January 23, 1976.

SHACKLETON'S WAY OF DEVELOPING LEADERSHIP SKILLS

(From 1914 to 1916, Sir Ernest Shackleton and his men survived the wreck of their ship, "Endurance," in the crushing Antarctic ice, stranded twelve hundred miles from civilization with no means of communication and no hope for rescue. The temperatures were so low the men could hear water freeze. They subsisted on a diet of penguins, dogs, and seals. And when the ice began to break up, Shackleton set out to save them all on his heroic eight-hundred mile trip across the frigid South Atlantic—in little more than a rowboat. Unlike most other polar expeditions, every man survived—not only in good health, but also in good spirits—all due to the leadership of Shackleton).

- Cultivate a sense of compassion and responsibility for others. You have a bigger impact on the lives
  of those under you than you can imagine.
- Once you make a career decision, commit to sticking through the tough learning period.
- Do your part to help create an upbeat environment at work. A positive and cheerful workplace is
  important to productivity.
- Broaden your cultural and social horizons beyond your usual experiences. Learning to see things from different perspectives will give you greater flexibility in problem solving at work.

- In a rapidly changing world, be willing to venture in new directions to seize new opportunities and learn new skills.
- Find a way to turn setbacks and failures to your advantage. This would be a good time to step forward on your own.
- Be bold in vision and careful in planning. Dare to try something new, but be meticulous enough in your proposal to give your ideas a good chance of succeeding.
- Learn from past mistakes—yours and those made by others. Sometimes the best teachers are the bad bosses and the negative experiences.
- Never insist on reaching a goal at any cost. It must be achieved at a reasonable expense, without undue hardship for your staff.
- Don't be drawn into public disputes with rivals. Rather, engage in respectful competition. You may need their cooperation some day.

Source: Margot Morrell and Stephanie Capparell. *Shackleton's Way.* New York: Viking Press 2001. p45.

Albert Schweitzer:
Albert Schweitzer was born on January 14, 1875 in Kayersburg, Germany. The eldest of his siblings, Schweitzer had a deeply religious family who lived in Upper Alsace Germany, now a part of France. He valued music and his Christian faith which taught him to be kind and generous to his fellow men. He studied organ music and became an accomplished organist by age 18. At 21, Schweitzer began learning all he could of science, music, and theology with the goal that by age 30, he could devote his life to humanitarian efforts. His desire was to be a doctor of medicine so that he could help the poor of the world. At the University of Strasbourg, he studied surgery for eight years while his wife Helene Bresslau studied nursing to assist him in his work. By age 38, Schweitzer and his wife set out as medical missionaries to Equatorial Africa (present-day Gabon). There he built a hospital and treated 2,000 poor African patients in his first year alone. His work was financed through gifts from people all over the world. By 1917, Schweitzer was arrested by the French, who were warring with Germany. Sent as a prisoner of war to France, he wrote *The Decay and the Restoration of Civilization and Ethics* during his imprisonment until 1918. Schweitzer made known his belief that civilization was being destroyed because people could not love. His suggestion that everyone develop a "reverence for life" meant all should

love and cherish every form of life. In 1924, Schweitzer returned to Africa and found his hospital in ruins. Two miles down the river he rebuilt it, again with gifts from people around the world. By 1963, the hospital had 350 beds with 150-bed leper colony. A staff of 36 doctors and other hospital workers assisted Schweitzer in his work. He made frequent trips to Europe during his life to raise money for his work through lectures and organ recitals. He wrote books on philosophy and theology, and made records to help fund his humanitarian work. Schweitzer's devotion to mankind won him many awards including the Queen of England's Order of Merit and the Nobel Peace Prize for 1952. His dedication to missionary work and humanitarian aid serve today as an inspiration (from www.norfacad.pvt.k12.va.us/project/schweitz/ life.htm, September 11, 2000).

Ignaz Philipp Semmelweis:

Born in 1818 and educated at Pest and Vienna universities, Semmelweis earned his Doctorate from Vienna in 1844 and became an assistant in the obstetric clinic in Vienna. He quickly became involved in the problem of puerperal ("childbed") infection, the scourge of numbers of maternal hospitals throughout Europe. At a time when women delivered at home, those who had to seek medical help from hospitals because of poverty, illegitimacy, or obstetrical complications faced high mortality raters, upwards of 25-30 percent. Thought circulated that the infection was caused by overcrowding, poor ventilation, the onset of lactation, or miasma. Semmelweis continued to investigate the cause of the infection among strong objections of his supervisor, who had reconciled himself to believe that the disease was unpreventable, as was the common thought of other physicians.

Semmelweis found that, among the women in the first section of the clinic, the death rate from childbed fever was two to three times as high as among those in the second section, although the two sections were identical with the exception that students were in the first and midwives in the second. He put forward the thesis that perhaps the students carried something to the patients they examined during labor. The death of a friend from a wound infection incurred during the examination of a woman who died of puerperal infection and the similarity of the findings in the two cases gave support to his reasoning. He concluded that students who came directly from the dissecting room to the maternity ward carried the infection from mothers who had died of the disease to healthy mothers. He ordered the students to wash their hands in a solution of chlorinated lime before each examination.

Under these procedures, the mortality rates in the first section dropped from 18.27 percent to 1.27 percent, and in March and August of 1848 no woman died in childbirth in his section. The younger medical men in Vienna recognized the significance of Semmelweis' discovery and gave him all possible assistance. His superior, on the other hand, was critical—not because he wanted to oppose him but because he failed to understand him.

In 1848, a liberal political revolution swept across Europe, and Semmelweis took part in the events of Vienna. After the revolution had been put down, Semmelweis found that his political activities had increased the obstacles to his professional work. In 1849, he was dropped from his post at the clinic. He then applied for a teaching post at the university midwifery but was turned down. Soon after that, he gave a successful lecture at the Medical Society of Vienna entitled "The Origin of Puerperal Fever." At the same time, he applied once more for the teaching post, but, although he received it, there were restrictions attached to it that he considered humiliating. He left Vienna and returned to Pest in 1850.

He worked for the next six years at the St. Rochus Hospital in Pest. An epidemic of puerperal fever had broken out in the obstetrics unit, and, at his request, Semmelweis was put in charge of the department. His measures promptly reduced the mortality rate, and in his years there it averaged only 0.85 percent. In Prague and Vienna, meantime, the rate was still from 10 to 15 percent.

In 1855, he was appointed professor of obstetrics at the University of Pest. He married, had five children, and developed his private practice. His ideas were accepted in Hungary, and the government addressed a circular to all district authorities ordering the introduction of the prophylactic methods of Semmelweis. In 1857, he declined the chair of obstetrics at the University of Zurich. Vienna remained hostile toward him, and the editor of the *Wiener Medizinische Wochenschrift* wrote that it was time to stop the nonsense about the chlorine hand wash.

Semmelweis published his principal work in 1861, *Die Ätiologie, der Begriff und die Prophylaxis des Kindbettfiebers* ("Etiology, Understanding, and Preventing of Childbed Fever"). He sent it to all the prominent obstetricians and medical societies abroad, but the general reaction was adverse. The weight of authority stood against his teachings. He addressed several open letters to professors of medicine in other countries, but to little effect. At a conference of German physicians and natural scientists, most of the speakers—including the pathologist Rudolf Virchow—rejected his doctrine. The years of controversy gradually undermined his spirit. In 1865, he suffered a breakdown and was taken to a mental hospital, where he died. Ironically, his illness and death were caused by the infection of a wound on his right hand, apparently the result of an operation he had performed before being taken ill. He died of the same disease against which he had struggled all his professional life.

Semmelweis' doctrine was subsequently accepted by medical science. His influence on the development of knowledge and control of infection was hailed by Joseph Lister, the father of modern antisepsis: "I think with the greatest admiration of him and his achievement and it fills me with joy that at last he is given the respect due to him" (from www.britannica.com/bcom/eb/article/5/0,5716,68445+1,00.html).

Babe Didrikson Zaharias:

Born in 1914 as Mildred Ella Didriksen in Galveston, Texas, Babe Didrikson was one of the greatest American athletes of the 20th century, excelling in golf, basketball, and track and field. From 1930-32, she was a member of the women's All-America basketball team, and also won eight events in national track and field. Didrikson joined the 1932 Olympic Games, hosted in Los Angeles and won the 80-meter hurdles and the javelin throw. She was an all-around athlete, participating in baseball, softball, swimming, billiards, figure skating, and even football.

Didrikson married George Zaharias, a professional wrestler, in 1938. Casually playing golf in 1932, she began playing exclusively in 1934. Restored to amateur status after going professional, Didrikson won the US Women's Amateur tourney in 1946. The following year, she won 17 straight championships in golf, including the British Ladies Amateur, of which she was the first United States holder. Turning professional again in 1948, she won the US Women's Open then and again in 1950. Overcoming a diagnosis of cancer in 1953, Didrikson went on clinch the US Open title again in 1954 (from britannica.com, 1999-2000).

A PRAYER

I asked God for strength, that I might achieve,
I was made weak, that I might learn humbly to obey…
I asked for health, that I might do greater things,
I was given infirmity, that I might do better things…
I asked for riches, that I might be happy,
I was given poverty, that I might be wise…
I ask for power, that I might have the praise of men,
I was given weakness, that I might feel the need of God…
I asked for all things, that I might enjoy life,
I was given life, that I might enjoy all things…
I got nothing that I asked for…but everything I had hoped for,
Almost despite myself, my unspoken prayers were answered.
I am among all men, most richly blessed.
--Prayer of an unknown Confederate soldier,
reprinted on the greeting cards of Democratic Presidential
candidate Adlai E. Stevenson, Christmas 1955[38]

Chapter Nine
Self-Affirmation Quotations

You must be the change you wish to see in the world.
--Mahatma Gandhi

This is the beginning of a new day. You have been given this day to use as you will. You can waste it or use it for good. What you do today is important because you are exchanging a day of your life for it. When tomorrow comes, this day will be gone forever; in its place is something that you have left behind...let it be something good.
--Author Unknown

Be glad of life, because it gives you the chance to love and to work and to play and to look up at the stars.
--Henry Van Dyke

Here is a test to find out whether your mission in life is complete. If you're alive, it isn't.
--Richard Bach, from the book *Illusions*

I would rather be ashes than dust! I would rather that my spark should burn out in a brilliant blaze than it should be stifled by dry rot. I would rather be a superb meteor, every atom of me in magnificent glow, than a sleepy and permanent planet. The proper function of man is to live, not to exist. I shall not waste my days in trying to prolong them. I shall use my time.
--Jack London

There is no such thing in anyone's life as an unimportant day.
--Alexander Woollcott

When you were born, you cried and the world rejoiced. Live your life so that when you die, the world cries and you rejoice.
--Cherokee Expression

Every blade of grass has its angel that bends over it and whispers, 'Grow, grow."
--The Talmud

If you cannot be a poet, be the poem
--David Caradine

To live content with small means; to seek elegance rather than luxury; and refinement rather than fashion; to be worthy, not respectable; and wealthy, not rich; to study hard, think quietly, talk gently, act frankly; to listen to stars and birds, to babes and sages, with open heart; to bear all cheerfully, do all bravely, await occasion, hurry never; in a word, to let the spiritual, unbidden, and unconscious grow up through the uncommon. This is to be my symphony.

--William Henry Channing

Don't ask yourself what the world needs; ask yourself what makes you come alive. And then go and do that. Because what the world needs is people who have come alive.

--Harold Whitman

O, with what freshness, what solemnity and beauty, is each new day born; as if to say to insensate man, 'Behold! Thou hast one more chance! Strive for immortal glory!'

--Harriet Beecher Stowe

Life is an opportunity, benefit from it.
Life is beauty, admire it.
Life is bliss, taste it.
Life is a dream, realize it.
Life is a challenge, meet it.
Life is a duty, complete it.
Life is a game, play it.
Life is a promise, fulfill it.
Life is a sorrow, overcome it.
Life is a song, sing it.
Life is a struggle, accept it.
Life is a tragedy, confront it.
Life is an adventure, dare it.
Life is luck, make it.
Life is too precious, do not destroy it.
Life is life, fight for it.

--Mother Teresa

There are only two ways to live your life. One is as though nothing is a miracle. The other is as if everything is.
>--Albert Einstein

All my life I've wanted to be somebody. But I see now I should have been more specific.
>--Jane Wagner

We are each of us angels with only one wing, and we can only fly by embracing one another.
>--Luciano de Crescenzo

Carpe Diem! Rejoice while you are alive; enjoy the day; live life to the fullest; make the most of what you have. It is later than you think.
>--Horace

To have striven, to have made an effort, to have been true to certain ideals—this alone is worth the struggle. We are here to add what we can to, not to get what we can from life.
>--Sir William Osler

You will find as you look back upon your life that the moments when you have truly lived are the moments when you have done things in the spirit of love.
>--Henry Drummond

We are more than what we do…much more than what we accomplish…far more than what we possess.
>--William Arthur Ward

What you possess in the world will be found at the day of your death to belong to someone else. But what you are, will be yours forever.
>--Henry Van Dyke

Life is not a 'brief candle.' It is a splendid torch that I want to make burn as brightly as possible before handing one to future generations.
>--George Bernard Shaw

To be always intending to make a new and better life but never to find time to set about it is as…to put off eating and drinking and sleeping from one day to the next until you're dead.

> --Og Mandino

Time is too slow for those who wait, too swift for those who fear, too long for those who grieve, too short for those who rejoice, but for those who love, time is eternity.

> --Henry Van Dyke

Gather ye rosebuds while ye may, old Time is still a-flying; And this same flower that smiles today, tomorrow will be dying.

> --Robert Herrick

Be such a man, and live such a life, that if every man were such as you, and every life a life like yours, this earth would be God's Paradise.

> --Phillips Brooks

Security is mostly a superstition. It does not exist in nature, nor do the children of men as a whole experience it. Avoiding danger is no safer in the long run than outright exposure. Life is either a daring adventure, or nothing.

> --Helen Keller

Nothing should be prized more highly than the value of each day.

> --Goethe

Do not believe in anything simply because you have heard it. Do not believe in anything simply because it is spoken and rumored by many. Do not believe in anything simply because it is found written in your religious books. Do not believe in anything merely on the authority of your teachers and elders. Do not believe in traditions because they have been handed down for many generations. But after observation and analysis, when you find that anything agrees with reason and is conducive to the good and benefit of one and all, then accept it and live up to it.

> --Buddha

You can't do anything about the length of your life, but you can do something about its width and depth.
--Shira Tehrani

May you live all the days of your life.
--Jonathan Swift

One SONG can spark a moment
One FLOWER can wake the dream
One TREE can start a forest
One BIRD can herald spring
One SMILE begins a friendship
One HANDCLASP lifts a soul
One STAR can guide a ship at sea
One WORD can frame the goal
One VOTE can change a nation
One SUNBEAM lights a room
One CANDLE wipes out darkness
One LAUGH will conquer gloom
One STEP must start each journey
One WORD must start a prayer
One HOPE will raise our spirits
One TOUCH can show you care
One VOICE can speak with wisdom
One HEART can know what's true
One LIFE can make a difference
--Author Unknown

After awhile you learn
The subtle difference between
Holding a hand and chaining a soul
And you learn that love doesn't mean possession
And company doesn't mean security.
And you begin to learn that kisses aren't contracts
And presents aren't promises and you begin to accept
Your defeats with your head up and your eyes ahead
With the grace of an adult not the grief of a child.
And you learn to build your roads today
Because tomorrow's ground is too uncertain for plans
And futures have ways of falling down in mid-flight.
After awhile you learn that even sunshine
Burns if you get too much so plant your
Own garden and decorate your own soul
Instead of waiting for someone to bring you flowers.
And you learn that you really can endure
That you really are strong
And you really do have worth
And you learn
And you learn…
--Veronica A. Shoffstall, "After a While" (copyright 1971)

It is not length of life, but depth of life.
--Ralph Waldo Emerson

For attractive lips, speaks words of kindness.
For lovely eyes, seek out the good in people.
For a slim figure, share your food with the hungry.
For beautiful hair, let a child run his fingers through it once a day.
For poise, walk with the knowledge you never walk alone.

We leave you a tradition of the future. The tender loving
Care of human beings will never become obsolete.

People, even more than things, have to be restored, renewed,
Revived, reclaimed, redeemed and redeemed and redeemed.
Never throw anyone away.

Remember, if you ever need a helping hand, you'll find
One at the end of your arm.

As you grow older, you'll discover that you have two hands:
One for helping yourself, the second for helping others.

You may have great days still ahead of you. May there be many of them
--Beauty Secrets (As published in a recent Dear Abby column, believed
to be the
poem Audrey Hepburn shared with her family shortly before she died.)

Seek the wisdom of the ages, but look at the world through the eyes of a
child.
--Ron Wild

Twenty years from now you will be more disappointed by the things that
you didn't do than by the one you did do. So throw off the bowlines. Sail
away from the safe harbor. Catch the trade winds in your sails. Explore.
Dream. Discover.
--Mark Twain

Look at everything as though you were seeing it either for the first or last
time. Then your time on earth will be filled with glory.
--Betty Smith

And in the end, it's not the years in your life that count. It's the life in your
years.
--Abraham Lincoln

We are not human beings on a spiritual journey. We are spiritual beings
on a human journey.
--Stephen Covey

The secret of health for both mind and body is not to mourn for the past,
not to worry about the future, or not to anticipate troubles, but to live in the
present moment wisely and earnestly.
--Buddha
(www. Inspirationpeak.com/life.html, 1999)

Chapter Ten
Handouts For Life

Three Things We *Know* About the Future

It is not going to be like the past.

It is not going to be exactly the way we think it is going to be.

The rate of change will take place faster than we imagine.

Take Time

Take time to **WORK**, it is the price of success.
Take time to **PLAY**, it is the secret of perpetual youth.
Take time to **THINK**, it is the source of power.
Take time to **READ**, it is the fountain of wisdom.
Take time to **WORSHIP**, it is the highway of
reverence.
Take time to **PRAY**, it is the greatest power on earth.
Take time to **LISTEN**, it is the pathway to
understanding.
Take time to **DREAM**, it is the music of the soul.
Take time to **LOVE** and be **LOVED**, it is the gift of
God.
--   Author Unknown

Failure Is Not an Event,
It's a Matter of Opinion

- Beethoven was such an awkward violinist that he gave up the instrument to write his own compositions.
- Winston Churchill did not become Prime Minister of England until he was sixty-two, after a lifetime of political defeats and setbacks.
- Louis Pasteur was a mediocre student, ranking fifteenth out of twenty-two chemistry students in his university studies.
- Leo Tolstoy, the author of *War and Peace*, flunked out of college.
- Albert Einstein did not speak until he was four years old and could not read until he was seven. His teacher described him as "mentally slow…adrift in foolish dreams."
- Henry Ford went bankrupt five times before succeeding as the world's best automobile maker and innovator.
- Abraham Lincoln was born into poverty, raised in obscurity, and failed in business. He ran for office and lost for the state legislature, the Congress, and the Senate before being elected President of the United States twice.

Courage

Why is it that most men's lives are controlled by small and petty circumstances? I am saddened as I watch people lose the good and great things that are within their reach and could be theirs with "but a little act of courage!"   -Author Unknown

Are You a Ty Cobb or
A Max Carey?

Every baseball fan knows that Ty Cobb was one of baseball's greatest players. His record for stealing bases stood for years. Cobb stole 96 bases the year he set the record.

Ask baseball fans if they know Max Carey and most of them will shake their heads and ask, "Who was Max Carey?" Carey, too, had baseball talent. In fact, one season he attempted 53 stolen bases and succeeded 51 times—an unbelievable 96 percent. Ty Cobb stole 96 bases the year he set the record, but he tried 134 times. That is only 71 percent. Cobb was willing to chance failure and because of it, he became legendary in the Baseball Hall of Fame. Max Carey, who played it safe time after time, is not remembered today.

Like Ty Cobb, you are going to make mistakes. But keep trying. If you win often enough, people will forget the times you failed. To succeed, you need to take risks. Don't always play it safe.

CLOSE is a way to describe failure and near success.

CLOSE is a synonym for the best in mediocrity; it is a contradiction and in reality cannot be.

CLOSE is when you almost care enough to want the very best.

There is a story of a boy's mother who called from the other room, "Marvin, are you spitting in the goldfish bowl?" And Marvin said, "No, but I'm coming pretty close!"

Misplaced Destiny

There is a Native American fable about a young brave who took an egg from an eagle's nest and put it in a chicken yard. The egg hatched and the eagle grew up among the chickens, pecking in the ground for food as they did, scratching the dust as he watched others do. One day he looked up and saw an eagle soaring above him. He felt his wings trembling as he said to one of the chickens, *"I wish I could do that."*

"Don't be a fool," the chicken said. *"Only an eagle can fly so high"* Feeling ashamed of his longing, the eagle went back to scratching in the dirt—never again to question what he believed to be an assigned place on earth.

It's all a matter of perception. Before the eagle could fly, he had to alter his perception of himself and recognize that he did not belong in the situation where circumstances had placed him. Only then was he ready to move on.

In My Library

"In my library there are about a thousand volumes of biography—a rough calculation indicates that more of these deal with men who have talked themselves upward than with all the scientist, writers, saints, and doers combined. Talkers have always ruled. They will continue to rule. The smart thing is to join them.

--Bruce Barton, 1886-1967

Scholar, editor, author, congressman, executive, and founder of the ad agency Batten, Durstine, and Osborn.

Bible Facts

The Bible consists of…
- 66 books
- 1,189 chapters
- 31,102 verses
- 775,639 words

It was written….
- By 40 different authors
- Over the course of 1500 years
- On three different continents

Other interesting facts:
- Longest chapter: Psalm 119
- Shortest chapter: Psalm 117
- Longest verse: Esther 8:9
- Shortest verse: John 11:39

How Soon We All Forget

People forget 40 percent
Of what you say to them
20 minutes later.

People forget 90 percent
In one week and
95 percent in two weeks.

However…
People will recall 60 percent
Of a message that is
Repeated six times.

In a Lifetime

During one's lifetime a person may be rated by the number who serve him, but after his passing he is measured by the number he served.

Napoleon made himself master of France and most of Europe by the power of his marching legions, but Louis Pasteur made himself the servant of France and the world in fighting the germs of disease, and Pasteur outlives Napoleon.

Mussolini dominated Italy for a decade, and was dishonored. Signor Marconi put his electrical wizardry at the service of his nation and the world and is still honored.

Some nations go into Africa to divide and dominate, while Albert Schweitzer devoted his life to healing the natives of Africa.

"Whosoever would be great among you,
let him be your servant."

Don't Quit

When things go wrong, as they sometimes will,
When the road you're trudging seems all uphill,
When the funds are low and the debts are high,
And you want to smile, but you have to sigh,
When care is pressing you down a bit,
Rest, if you must, —but don't you quit.

Life is queer with its twists and turns,
As every one of us sometimes learns,
And many a failure turns about
When he might have won had he stuck it out;
Don't give up, though the pace seems slow—
You might succeed with another blow.

Often the goal is nearer than
It seems to a faint and faltering man,
Often the struggler has given up
When he might have captured the victor's cup.
And he learned too late, when the night slipped down,
How close he was to the golden crown.

Success is failure turned inside out—
The silver tint of the clouds of doubt—
And you never can tell how close you are,
It may be near when it seems afar;
So stick to the fight when you're hardest hit—
It's when things seem worst that you mustn't quit
--Anonymous

Sermons We See

I'd rather see a sermon than hear one any day.
I'd rather one should walk with me than merely show
the way.

The eye's a better pupil and more willing than the ear;
Fine counsel is confusing, but example is always clear.

And best of all the preachers are the men who live their
creeds,
For to see the good in action is what everybody needs.

I can soon learn how to do it if you'll let me see it done;
I can watch your hands in action, but your tongue too
fast may run.

And lectures you deliver may be very wise and true,
But I would rather get my lesson by observing what
you do.

For I may misunderstand you and the high advice you
give,
But there's no misunderstanding how you act and how
you live.
--Edgar A. Guest

I want you to face the mountain
So that you can see,
When the mountain is out of the way—
All that is left is me.

Only I can move the mountain,
Only I can push it away,
Only I can conquer the problems
That you face today.

Your only job is to believe,
To listen to my voice,
And when you hear what I command,
Obedience is your choice.

But I will not make it too difficult
For the victory
Is already mine, and I
Will fill you with my spirit
And through you my grace will shine.

Not when you are perfect,
Like you think you need to be,
But when your heart is willing
To become more and more like me.

Old Phrases

Here are some common phrases used every day.
See if you have any idea where they came from.

"Thanks for nothing."
"No limits but the sky."
"To give the devil his due."
"A peck of trouble."
"Let the worst come to the worst."
"A finger in every pie."
"Every dog has his day."
"A wild goose chase."

Give up? Every one of them appeared in one book.
Don Quixote, written more than 350 years ago by
Miguel de Cervantes.

Plan BACKWARDS

Planning backward
Contains the idea of a specific goal.
You choose a goal,
Picture yourself accomplishing it
Then plan backward until you know
Exactly where and when
You must start."

--Norman Vincent Peale

The Gist of the Books of the Bible

Genesis
God at work / Everything begins here
Exodus
Free at last / The slaves of Egypt get a liberator
Leviticus
Living with fire / Dangerous material more powerful than atom
Numbers
Forty years of misery / A joyous adventure comes to a tragic end
Deuteronomy
A personal plea / Moses' last chance with the people of Israel
Joshua
The difference 40 years can make / Facing overwhelming odds with renewed hope
Judges
Freedom fighters / Judges who took up arms to defend their homeland
Ruth
A rare bond of love / Ruth and Naomi lost everything, except their care for each other
I Samuel
What leadership requires / Israel, fighting for survival, needed a leader
II Samuel
The life of King David / From herding sheep to ruling a nation
I Kings
The man who had everything / The richest, wisest, most successful person of his time
II Kings
The great wars of Israel / The promised land turns into a bloody battlefield
I Chronicles
A family record / These facts reminded Israelites of the place in God's plan
II Chronicles
A time for hope / Restoring pride in a group of refugees

Ezra
Beginning again / For the exiles from Babylon, news almost too good
to be true
Nehemiah
A man of action / He set out to build a wall but left an enduring legacy
of leadership
Esther
A profile of courage / Heroes act while others stand and watch
Job
When bad things happen to a good person / Noboby suffered more or
deserved it less
Psalms
Cries from the heart / Songs of sorrow as well as joy
Proverbs
Uncommon sense / A most down to earth book
Ecclesiastes
When life seems senseless / A book for our time
Song of Songs
An intoxicating love / A poem about love the way it's meant to be
Isaiah
Prophet, poet, politician / His nation at a crossroads, Isaiah rose to meet
the challenge
Jeremiah
God's reluctant messenger / Jeremiah felt scared, insecure, but burned
with a message
Lamentations
A city in ruins / There was nothing left to do but weep
Ezekiel
Seeing the unseen God / God showed Himself to Ezekiel in unearthly
radiance
Daniel
Kidnapped / Even as prime minister, Daniel remained a lonely outsider
Hosea
Tearing God's heart / Why would he love such a woman?
Joel
The meaning of a natural disaster / What's behind a devastating locust
plague?

Amos
JUSTICE! / A simple farmer takes on a materialistic nation
Obadiah
Poetic justice / Obadiah gave the final word on a blood feud
Jonah
Good news for the enemy? / Jonah balked at loving the cruel Assyrians
Micah
Light in a dark time / Evil and violence were creeping south toward
Jerusalem
Nahum
God's answer to injustice / A power above the powers
Habakkuk
Problem with evil / Habakkuk's question "Why is God silent while the
wicked succeed?"
Zephaniah
Beyond darkness / A worldwide catastrophe and a shining light
Haggai
The prophet who got results / For once—God's people listened
Malachi
When faith grows weary / Malachi spoke to the people "going through
the motions"
Matthew
A bridge from old to new / Why start with a list of names?
Mark
The fast paced gospel / Mark reads like the script of an action movie
Luke
Like a joy-filled musical / Something was brewing on planet earth
John
God breaks the silence / He spoke in the only way we could truly
understand
Acts
The linking book / Imagine a Bible filled without the book of Acts
Romans
A most demanding audience / Stranded on an island, you'd want this
book!
I Corinthians
The last place to start a church / Few expected much from crazy
Corinth

II Corinthians
A book of joy and sadness / Why isn't Paul celebrating his victory?
Galatians
No second class Christians / A protest against treason
Ephesians
For the discouraged / Good news for those who feel abandoned and unloved
Philippians
Cheerful sounds from a jail cell / Joy when it's least expected
Colossians
Battling of the cults / For everything worthwhile, there exists a counterfeit
I Thessalonians
What made Paul successful / Apostle fusses over the city that once chased him away
II Thessalonians
A patient who didn't follow orders / When good advice goes ignored
I Timothy
The hardest job / Timothy steps into a hornet's nest
II Timothy
Passing the torch / The apostle Paul's last known words
Titus
Diverse people, diverse problems / A band of liars, brutes, and gluttons
Philemon
Letter to a slave owner / A slave's life hangs in the balance
Hebrews
Time to decide / Does it matter what you believe as long as you're sincere?
James
Words are not enough / You can believe all the right things yet still be dead wrong
I Peter
A word about suffering / What to do when trouble comes
II Peter
A threat from within / The worst dangers aren't always well marked
I John
Words that get polluted / A problem with a new generation

I Will Do It Someday

I will do it
Someday when I am older
Someday when I have more education
Someday when I have enough money
Someday when I know the right people
Someday when I am skinny
Someday when I have a tan
Someday when I am not so tired
Someday when I have the time
BUT
Someday I will be dead.

On Top of the World

In the Tate Gallery in London is Frederic Watt's famous
painting, "Hope."
There is a delicate, lovely woman seated upon a globe.
Her head is bowed and her eyes are blindfolded,
As if stricken and dejected.
She holds in her hand a harp with only one string,
Which is stretched to the snapping point –
All others have already broken;
And her hand touches that one string – hope – and,
With head bent, toward it to catch the sweet melody,
She plays music, sweet, soulful and satisfying.
In that simple and profound presentation there is pathos and
tenderness.
When your little world stops turning and
Your own personal sun quits shining,
How wonderful that hope can take up life's harp
And play upon the one remaining string.
When you do that, there is still a chance for you.

You are writing a gospel,
A chapter each day;
By deeds you do;
By words you say;
Men read and write,
Whether faulty or true,
Say what is the gospel
According to you?
--Unknown

An Uncommon Skill
The Bible says, "Let us speak the truth in love."

Have you ever seriously considered how difficult a task that really is?

The great French statesman Richelieu built a reputation as a man capable of speaking in love. In fact, the story is told of a young man who applied to Richelieu for a job, knowing all along his request would be turned down. Richelieu exhibited a manner of speech that was warm and accepting. Those closest to him said it was worth having a request denied just to hear how graciously he expressed himself. Even when he gave out bad news, it was easy to accept.

(Richelieu's sweet spirit proved it's not what we say but how we say it that really counts.)

The Fear of Failure

You've failed many times, although you may not remember.
You fell down the first time you tried to walk. Did you hit the
ball the first time you swung a bat? Heavy hitters, the ones who
hit the most home runs, also strike out a lot.

**English novelist John Creasey got 753 rejection slips
before he published 564 books.**

**Babe Ruth struck out 1,330 times, but he also hit 714
home runs.**

Don't worry about failure.
Focus on the chances you miss when you don't even try!

St. John's: A College That Works

"You can tell whether a man is clever by his answers. You can tell whether a man is wise by his questions." -- Naguid Mahfouz

St. John's College has roughly 400 students who attend each of the two campuses in Annapolis, Maryland, and Santa Fe, New Mexico. The administration has the strange idea that some writers and some books are better than others, so rather than let students pick and choose, they serve the same menu to everyone – Greek, French, music, math, and science – in a four-year great books diet of Plato, Dante, Bacon, Hume, Kant, Kierkeguard, Einstein, WEB DuBois, and Booker T. Washington.

According to an article in the *American Way* magazine, St. John's holds fast to the medieval notion that all knowledge is one and to the Renaissance man ideas that a truly educated person knows a lot about a lot. Even stranger, there are no final examinations, no professional training, few intercollegiate athletics, no fraternities or sororities, and almost no electives. Even more peculiar, all St. John's tutors are prepared to teach all the books from Euclid on geometry to Machiavelli on politics and Hiesenberg on quantum mechanics. St. Johns' forces students to bear major responsibility for their education. The teaching or tutoring sessions are mostly open for discussions, with every student expressing opinions, introducing ideas, and stimulating thought. They believe that we learn things together, that we don't learn alone. The books they use are terribly hard, and "you use the other people in the class to help you understand."

Does it work? Yes, seventy percent of the graduates go on to graduate school within five years of graduation, and the school ranks fifth nationally in the number of graduates earning doctorates in humanities.

Roughly 19 percent of St. John's grads become teachers or administrators. Twenty-seven percent are scattered across the professional spectrum, working in government, public affairs, computer science, engineering, and so on. Another 20 percent go on to law school, and almost seven percent go into health and medical professions.

If you can read and don't, you're no better off than the person who can't read at all.

Character:

The aggregate of features and traits that form
the apparent individual nature of some person or thing;

Qualities of honesty, courage, or the like;

Integrity;

Reputation;

Good repute;

An account of the moral qualities, ethical standards,
principles;

The distinctive qualities that make one recognizable
as a person differentiated from others.[39]

Success

Mother Teresa attended a gathering with kings
And presidents and statesmen from all over the world.
They were there in their crowns and jewels and silks
And Mother Teresa wore her sari held together by a
Safety pin.

One of the noblemen spoke to her of her work
With the poorest of the poor in Calcutta. He asked her
If she didn't become discouraged because she saw so
Few successes in her ministry. Mother Teresa
answered,
"No, I do not become discouraged. You see, God has
not called me to a ministry of success. He has called
me to a ministry of mercy."[40]

Bullets or Seeds

Richard C. Halverson
Former chaplain of the United States Senate

You can offer your ideas to others as bullets or seeds.
You can shoot them, sow them; hit people in the head with
them, or plant them in their hearts.
Ideas used as bullets will kill inspiration and neutralize
motivation. Used as seeds, they take root, grow, and become
reality in the life in which they are planted.

The only risk in the seed approach: Once it grows and
becomes part of those in whom it's planted, you probably will
get no credit for originating the idea. But if you're willing to do
without the credit, you'll reap a rich harvest.[41]

Lessons From Geese

1. As each bird flaps its wings, it creates an "uplift" for the bird following. By flying in a "V" formation, the whole flock adds 71% greater flying range than if the bird flew alone.
   Lesson: People who share a common direction and sense of community can get where they are going quicker and easier because they are traveling on the thrust of one another.

2. Whenever a goose falls out of formation, it suddenly feels the drag and resistance of trying to fly alone, and quickly gets back into formation to take advantage of the "lifting power" of the bird immediately in front.
   Lesson: If we have as much sense as a goose, we will stay in formation with those who are headed where we want to go (and be willing to accept their help as well as give ours to others).

3. When the lead goose gets tired, it rotates back into the formation and another goose flies at point position.
   Lesson: It pays to take turns doing the hard tasks and share leadership with people, as with geese, we are interdependent on each other.

4. The geese in formation honk from behind to encourage those up front to keep up their speed.
   Lesson: we need to make sure our honking from behind is encouraging – and not otherwise
   .

5. When a goose gets sick or wounded or shot down, two geese drop out of formation and follow it down to help and protect it. They stay with it until it is able to fly again or dies. Then they launch out on their own, with another formation, or catch up with the flock.
   Lesson: If we have as much sense as a goose, we too will stand by each other in difficult times as well as when we are strong.

Knowledge

Books extend our narrow present back into the limitless past. They show us the mistakes of the men and women before us and share with us recipes for human success. There's nothing to be done which books will not help us do better.

It is estimated that the average person adds only fives words a year to his vocabulary. You should add that many per week.

With wisdom and knowledge come kindness, patience, love, understanding, and success as a person.

Neil Armstrong's vision began as a lad. In an interview immediately following his historic first step on the moon, he said, "Ever since I was a little boy, I dreamed I would do something important in aviation."

Some years ago, *Reader's Digest* told of a class of high school basketball players with similar skills who were divided into three separate groups to conduct an experiment. Group One was told not to practice shooting free throws for one month. Group Two was told to practice shooting free throws in the gym every afternoon for an hour for a month. Group Three was told to practice shooting free throws in their imaginations every afternoon for one hour for one month The results? Group One slipped slightly in the percentage free throw average; Group Two increased about two percentage points; and Group Three increased two percentage points. Ridiculous! How could your free throw average improve as much from practicing in your imagination as from actual practice in the gym? Simply because in your imagination you never miss, unless you want to, or unless its your habit.

Read about those who are successful, imagine yourself in various biographies about people who began with little or in some case, nothing. Remember, what you see is what you will be, and the quickest way to intelligence is through reading.

Expectations

Nell Mohney, in her book *Beliefs Can Influence Attitudes*, pointedly illustrates this truth. Mohney tells of a double-blind experiment conducted in the San Francisco Bay area. The principal of a school called three professors together and said, "Because you three teachers are the finest in the system and you have the greatest expertise, we're going to give you ninety high-IQ students. We're going to let you move these students through this next year at their own pace and see how much they can learn.

Everyone was delighted – faculty and students alike.

Over the next year, the professors and the students thoroughly enjoyed themselves. The professors were teaching the brightest students; the students were benefiting from the close attention and instruction of highly-skilled teachers. By the end of the experiment, the students had achieved from 20 to 30 percent more than the other students in a whole area.

The principal called the teachers in and told them, "I have a confession to make. You did not have ninety of the most intellectually prominent students. They were run-of-the-mill students. We took ninety students at random from the system and gave them to you."

The teachers said, "This means that we're exceptional teachers."

The principal continued, "I have another confession. You're not the brightest of teachers. Your names were the first three drawn out of a hat."

The teacher asked, "What made the difference? Why did ninety students perform at such an exceptional level for a whole year?"

The difference, of course, was the teachers' expectations. Our expectations have a great deal to do with our attitudes. And these expectations may be totally false, but they will determine our attitudes.[42]

William the Conqueror

William the Conqueror decided to back himself into a corner when he successfully invaded England. He burned his boats on the beaches as soon as he landed, leaving his armies no escape. Then he HAD to win; and he didn't have to think of a way out if he lost - - -
There WAS no way out!

Do It Now

If you have hard work to do, *do it now*.
Today the skies are clear and blue,
Tomorrow clouds may come in view
Yesterday is not for you, *do it now*.

If you have a song to sing, *sing it now*.
Let the tones of gladness ring
Clear as a song bird in spring.
Let each day some music bring: *sing it now*.

If you have kinds words to say, *say them now*.
Tomorrow may not come your way.
Do a kindness while you may,
Loved ones will not always stay; *say them now*.

If you have a smile to show, *show it now*.
Make hearts happy, roses grow,
Let the friends around you know
The love you have before they go, *show it now*.

Entrepreneur's Creed

I do not choose to be a common man.
It is my right to be uncommon, if I can.
I seek opportunity—not security.
I do not wish to be a kept citizen,
Humbled and dulled by having the state look after me.
I want to take calculated risk,
To dream and to build,
To fail and to succeed.
I refuse to barter incentive for a dole.
I prefer to challenges of life
To the guaranteed existence.
The thrill of fulfillment
To the calm state of Utopia.
I will not trade freedom for beneficence,
Nor my dignity for a handout.
It is my heritage to think
And act for myself.
And enjoy the benefit of my creations.
To face the world boldly and say
"This, with God's help, I have done."
All this is what means to be
An entrepreneur.
--Author Unknown

Obituary of John Averageman[43]

To whom it may concern:

John Averageman was buried today.

Born: 1903 into an averave family.
Schooling: attended grade and high school and managed to graduate without distinction. Voted most likely to remain average.
Married: 1924 Mary Mediocre.
Children: John Averageman Jr. and Mary Mediocre Averageman.
Employment: 42 years of undistinguished service to the Mediocre Products Co. John held several unimportant positions and managed to turn out mediocre products which brought him an average livelihood.
Biography: John Averageman never took a chance. He managed to develop practically none of his talents or abilities. He never became involved in anything or with anyone. His favorite book was "Non-Involvement": The Story of Playing it Safe.
Achievements: Lived 65 years without Goals, Plans, Desires, Confidence, or Determination.
Burial Arrangements: John's remains will rest undisturbed by the visits of friends in the Ordinary Man's Cemetery.

HERE LIES

Mr. john averageman
Born: 1903
Died: 1924
Buried: 1968

"He tried never to try."
"He asked little of life: Life paid his price."

Chapter Eleven
The Mini-Dictionary

Abate (uh-BATE): v. to put an end to; to reduce in intensity, amount, our value

Aberration (ab-uh-RAY-shun): n. a deviation from the normal, the usual, or the natural way; unsoundness or disorder of the mind

Abort (uh-BORT): v. To stop in the early stages; the bring forth prematurely; to end pregnancy before term

Abstraction (ab-STRAK-shun): n. a summary or picture that makes no attempt at precise representation.

Abyss (uh-BIS): n. bottomless or immeasurably deep gulf or pit

Accolade (AK-uh-lade): n. a mark or expression of praise

Acrid (AK-rid): adj. unpleasantly strong in taste or odor; very bitter

Acquisitor (uh-KWIZ-ut-er): n. someone who has acquired, especially library materials by purchase, exchange, or gift

Acrimony (AK-ruh-moe-nee): n. harshly or bitingly sharp words or manner

Acronym (AK-ruh-nim): n. a word formed from the first letter or letters of each word (or part) of a multi-word term

Activist (AK-ti-vist): adj. acting strongly in support of or in opposition to one side of a controversial issue

Acuity (a-KYU-it-ee): n. keeness of perception

Ad lib (ad-LIB): n. something spoken, composed, or performed without preparation

Adamant (AD-uh-munt): adj. unshakable or unmovable, especially in opposition

Admonish (ad-MON-ish): v. to warn or disapprove gently; to tell of duties or obligations

Admonition (ad-muh-NISH-un): n. gentle warning or disapproval

Adulation (aj-uh-LAY-shun): n. excessive or slavish flattery or admiration

Adversary (AD-ver-sair-ee): n. enemy or opponent

Adversity (ad-VER-si-tee): n. condition of suffering, illness, or poverty; a calamitous or disastrous experience

Affable (AF-uh-bull): adj. pleasant and at ease in talking to others; friendly

Afflict (uh-FLIKT): v. to distress to the point of persistent suffering or anguish

Aftermath (AF-ter-math): n. result; period after a usually ruinous event

Agonize (AG-uh-nize): v. to suffer agony; to cause agony

Alleged (uh-LEJD, uh-LEJ-uhd): adj. said to be true or to exist; questionably true or as specified

Allegory (AL-uh-gor-ee): n. the telling of truths or generalizations about human experience through symbolic fictional characters and actions; a symbolic representation

Alleviate (uh-LEE-vee-ate): v. to partially remove or correct; to make more bearable

Altruistic (al-tru-IS-tik): adj. unselfishly devoted to the welfare of others

Amalgam (uh-MAL-gam): n. mixture of different elements

Ambivalence (am-BIV-uh-lunss): n. simultaneous attraction and revulsion; continual fluctuation; uncertainty as to which approach to follow

Amorphous (uh-MORE-fuss): adj. having no definite shape, character, or nature; lacking organization or unity

Analogous (uh-NAL-uh-guss): adj. showing a resemblance in some ways even though being otherwise unlike

Anathema (un-NATH-uh-muh): n. a curse; someone cursed by church authorities; someone who is intensely disliked

Anguish (ANG-gwish): n. extreme pain in body or mind

Animosity (an-uh-MAHSS-utt-ee): n. ill will or resentment tending toward active hostility

Annexation (an-ek-SAY-shun): n. the attachment of one thing to another

Annihilate (uh-NY-uh-late): v. to destroy; to cease to exist; to cause to be of no effect

Anodyne (AN-uh-dine): n. something that soothes or comforts; a drug that allays pain

Anomaly (uh-NAHM-uh-lee): n. deviation from what is normal or common

Anonymity (an-uh-NIM-uht-tee): n. the quality of having or giving no name

Antagonize (an-TAG-uh-nize): v. to act in opposition to; to provoke hostility

Ante (ANT-ee): n. an amount paid

Apathy (AP-uh-thee): n. lack of feeling or emotion; lack of interest or concern

Apocalypse (uh-POCK-uh-lips): n. time when God will destroy the rulers of evil and raise the righteous to heaven; something seen as a prophetic revelation

Apotheosis (uh-pahth-ee-OH-sus): n. (pl. apotheoses) elevation to divine status; a perfect example

Appalling (uh-PAWL-ing) adj. causing horror, dismay, or disgust

Appreciable (uh-PREE-shuh-buhl): adj. able to be measured

Approbation (ap-ruh-BAY-shun): n. formal or official approval or praise

Arbitrary (AHR-buh-trair-ee): adj. selected at random and without reason; behaving unjustly and oppressively; capricious or high-banded

Arcane (ahr-KANE): adj. known only to one who has the key; secret, mysterious, supernatural

Argot (AHR-gut, AHR-go): n. a more or less secret dialect

Articulate (ahr-TIK-yuh-late): v. to utter distinctly and clearly; to unite by means of a joint; to form or fit into a systematic whole

Aspect (ASS-pekt): n. appearance; particular way in which something may be looked at

Aspirant (ASS-puh-runt, uh-SPY-runt): n. one who seeks a desired position or status

Assess (uh-SESS): v. to determine the rate, amount, size, value, or importance of; to impose or subject to a tax; to evaluate property in order to tax it

Assimilate (uh-SIM-uh-late): v. to absorb into the system, especially as nourishment, or into the group or culture; to take into the mind and understand thoroughly; to make similar

Assuage (uh-SWAYJ): v. to lessen pain or distress; to quiet; to put an end to by satisfying

Attaché (at-uh-SHAY, AT-TA-shay): n. technical expert attached to a foreign wing of his country's diplomatic staff

Attributable (uh-TRIB-yuht-uh-bul): adj. able to be regarded as belonging to a person or thing

Audacious (aw-DAY-shuss): adj recklessly bold or daring; contemptuous of law, religion, or decorum; marked by lively originality

Augur (AW-guhr): v. to foretell the future, especially from omens; to give promise

Augment (awg-MENT): v. to add to something that is already well or adequately developed

Austere (aw-STEER): adj. appearing stern and forbidding; unadorned, simple; somber

Authenticator (aw-THENNT-I-kay-tuhr): n. something that proves the truth or genuineness of something else

Autonomous (aw-TAWN-uh-muss): adj. marked by or having the right of self-government; existing; capable of existing, or being carried on independently, without outside control

Avatar (AV-uh-tahr): n. an incarnation in human form; an embodiment; one version or phase of a continuing entity

Backlash (BAK-lash): n. sudden violent backward movement; strong negative reaction

Banal (buh-NAL, BANE-uhl): adj. lacking originality; common, ordinary

Bastion (BASS-chun): n. a projecting part of a fortification; a fortified area; a stronghold

Belie (beh-LIE): v. to give a false impression; to contrast with; to contradict

Bellicose (BELL-ih-kose): adj. favoring or inclined to start wars or quarrels

Belligerent (buh-LIDJ-uh-runt): adj. waging war; hostile, warlike

Beneficiary (ben-uh-FISH-ee-ary): n. one who benefits from something; person named to receive benefits, especially monetary

Beset (bih-SET): v. to trouble, set upon, or hem in

Bifurcate (BY-fuhr-kate, by-FUHR-kate): v. to divide into two branches or parts

Bilateral (by-LAT-uh-ruhl, by-LATT-ruhl): adj. having two sides; affecting two sides or parties

Bland adj. smooth and soothing; showing no personal concern or embarrassment; dull

Blatant (BLATE-nt): adj. offensively noisy; offensively conspicuous

Blitzkrieg (BLITS-kreeg): n. war conducted with great speed or force; sudden or violent overpowering bombardment

Bogus (BOW-guss): adj. not genuine

Boisterous (BOY-struhss): adj. rowdy, stormy, marked by exuberant high spirits

Bolster (BOWL-ster): v. to support; to boost

Boycott (BOY-cot): n. refusal by a group to have dealings with, usually to show disapproval or to force acceptance of certain conditions

Bristle (BRISS-uhl): v. to take on an aggressive attitude or appearance

Broach v. to open up or break into; to open a subject for discussion

Bruit about (BREWT-uh-BOWT): v. to tell and retell a rumor or report

Bumbling (BUM-buh-ling): adj. stumbling; speaking in a faltering or stuttering way

Buoy (BOO-ee, BOY): v. to keep afloat; to support; to raise someone's spirits

Burnish (BUHRN-ish): v. to rub with a smoothing tool; to make shiny, especially by rubbing

Calamitous (kuh-LAM-uht-uss): adj. causing or being accompanied by major misfortune, great loss, or lasting misery

Candor (KAN-duhr, KAN-dore): n. honesty, sincerity; openness; freedom from prejudice or malice

Cap v. to provide with a cap; to outdo

Cardinal (KARD-nuhl, KARD-un-uhl): adj. of basic importance

Careen (ka-REEN): v. to sway from side to side

Cataclysmic (kat-uh-KLIZ-mik): adj. disastrous, marked by overwhelming upheaval and demolition

Catalytic (kat-uhl-IT-k): adj. causing or involving an action or reaction between persons or forces, in which the causer is unchanged by the reaction

Causal (CAW-zuhl): adj. arising from a cause; showing cause

Centenary (sen-TEN-uh-ree, SENT-uhn-er-ee): n. hundredth anniversary

Chagrined (shuh-GRINND): v. acutely disappointed or embarrassed

Chestnut (CHES-nutt): n. an old joke or story; something that has been repeated so often it is stale.

Chicanery (shik-AYN-uh-ree): n. trickery; a trick

Chronic (KRONN-ik): adj. marked by long duration, frequent occurrence; ever-present; done through habit

Circumspection (suhr-kum-SPEK-shun): n. consideration of all possible consequences and circumstances; cautiousness

Circumvent (suhr-kuhm-VENT): v. to detour around, to hem in, to stop or defeat with ingenuity or strategy

Clout (KLOWT): n. a blow with the hand; influence

Coherent (ko-HERE-ent): adj. holding together, being logically consistent, making sense

Cohesive (ko-HE-sivv): adj. tightly sticking together

Coincide (ko-uhn-SIDE): v. to occupy the same space or time; to be in agreement

Collateral (kuh-LATT-uh-ruhl): adj. accompanying but subordinate; serving to support or reinforce; indirect

Colloquial (kuh-LOH-kwee-uhl): adj. conversational; used in or characteristic of informal conversation

Comply (kum-PLY): v. to conform or adapt one's actions

Conciliatory (kuhn-SILL-yuh-tor-ee): adj. attempting to please to gain good will; being friendly or agreeable

Condescending (kahn-di-SEN-ding): adj. assuming an air of superiority; descending to a less dignified level

Confrontation (kahn-fruhn-TAY-shun): n. face-to-face meeting; clash of forces or ideas

Congenital (kuhn-JEN-uh-tuhl): adj. existing at or from birth; being such by nature; developed in the uterus rather than by heredity

Conjecture (kuhn-JEK-chuhr): n. conclusion made on slight grounds or by guesssswork

Consecrate (KAHN-suh-krate): v. to devote to a sacred purpose; to devote to a purpose with deep dedication; to make sacred or venerable

Contentious (kuhn-TEN-shuss): adj. likely to cause argument; enjoying argument

Context (KAHN-tekts): n. surrounding words that can throw light on a passage's meaning; surroundings

Contingent (kuhn-TIN-junt): adj. likely to happen; happening by chance; dependent on something else

Contingent n. troop

Contretemps (KAHN-truh-tahnh): n. (sing or pl.) an embarrassing or inconvenient occurrence

Contrition (kuhn-TRISH-uhn): n. the act of becoming sorry for sins or shortcomings

Convoluted (KAHN-vuh-loot-uhd): adj. folded in curved or twisted windings; twisted, intricate, or involved

Co-opt (koh-OPT): v. to take into a groups; to take over

Cordon off (KORD-n-awff): v. to form a restrictive line around something

Cornerstone (KOR-nuhr-stone): n. the most basic element

Cosmetic (koz-MET-ik): adj. beautifying; correcting defects, especially superficial ones

Coup (KOO): n. a brilliant, sudden, and usually very successful act

Credible (KRED-uh-buhl): adj. offering reasonable grounds for being believed

Crocodile (KROCK-uh-dile): adj. showing false sorrow (from crocodile tears, meaning false or affected tears)

Crudity (KROOD-uh-tee): n. vulgarity; state of being rude or uncultured

Cuckold (KUHK-uhld): n. a man whose wife is unfaithful

Cull (KULL): v. to select from a group

Culpable (KUHL-puh-buhl): adj. worthy of blame for acting wrong or harmfully

Curb (KERB): v. to furnish with a curb; to check or control

Curtail (ker-TAIL): v. to make less, to cut short

Debrief (dih-BREEF, dee-BREEF): v. to question in order to obtain useful information; to instruct not to reveal any classified information after release from a sensitive position

Default (dih-FAWLT): v. to fail to perform, pay, or make good; to forfeit a contest by such failure

Deficit (DEFF-uh-suht): n. a deficiency or loss in amount or quality; a business loss; a disadvantage

Defile (dih-FILE, dee-FILE): v. to corrupt; to make physically or ceremonially unclean or impure

Deftly adv. skillfully

Degenerate (dih-JEN-uh-ruht): adj. having declined from an ancestral or former state; having sunk to a lower, usually corrupt and vicious condition; having gotten worse or gone wrong

Demean (dih-MEEN): v. to lower in status; belittle

Demeanor (dih-MEEN-or): n. outward manner; outward behavior toward others

Denunciation (dih-NUN-see-AY-shun): n. act of publicly condemning or accusing

Deployment (dih-PLOY-munt): n. placement in battle formation; act of being used, arranged, or spread out, especially strategically

Derelict (DEHR-uh-likt): adj. abandoned, especially by the owner or occupant; lacking a sense of duty

Derelict n. castoff, outcast, or bum

Derisive (dih-RY-sihv): adj. expressing or causing ridicule or scorn

Desiccate (DESS-ih-kate): v. to dry up, to preserve by drying, to become dried up; to become drained of emotional or intellectual vitality

Desultory (DESS-uhl-tore-ee, DEZ, uhl-tore-ee): marked by lack of definite plan, regularity, or purpose; not connected with the main subject

Détente (day-TAHNHT): n. relaxation or strained relations or tensions

Deter (dih-TUHR): v. to turn aside, discourage, or prevent from acting

Detrimental (deh-truh-MENT-uhl): adj. obviously harmful

Detritus (dih-TREE-tuss): n. sing. or pl. a product (especially loose material) resulting from disintegration or wearing away

Differentiate (diff-uh-REN-chee-ate): v. to develop or show a difference; to recognize a difference

Dilatory (DILL-uh-to-ree): adj. tending or intended to cause delay; being delayed or put off

Diligent (DILL-uh-juhnt): adj. showing steady, earnest, energetic effort

Dint: n. force (by dint of : because of)

Disavow (dis-uh-VOW): v. to refuse to acknowledge; to deny responsibility for

Disciple (diss-I-puhl): n. a follower, a person who helps spread someone else's ideas

Disclaimer (diss-KLAY-muhr): n. a denial of legal claim; a formal refusal, denial, or surrendering of rights

Disconcerting (diss-kuhn-SER-ting): adj. disturbing the composure or throwing into confusion; embarrassing

Disparity (diss-PAR-uh-tee): n. difference

Dissident (DISS-uh-duhnt): n. one who disagrees with an opinion or a group

Dissuade (diss-WADE): v. to advise someone against something; to turn away by persuasion

Divergent (duh-VUHRJ-uhnt): adj. differing from each other or from a standard

Diverting (duh-VUHRT-ing): adj. pleasing, especially by distracting attention from what burdens or distresses

Divisive (duh-VI-sivv, duh-VISS-iv): adj. creating disunity or disagreement

Doddering (DODD-uh-ring): adj. old and feeble, senile, foolish

Domineering (dom-uh-NEAR-ing): adj. assuming strong and arbitrary control over another; tyrannizing

Drab: adj. dull brown in color; monotonously dull

Dubious (DYU-bee-us): adj. giving rise to doubt, undecided in opinion; doubtful or undecided in outcome, of questionable value or origin

Duplicitous (dyu-PLISS-uht-uss): adj. using deceptive words or actions to mask one's true intentions

Eclipse (ih-KLIPS): v. reduce in importance or reputation; obscure or darken

Ecological (ee-kuh-LODJ-ih-kuhl): adj. having to do with the relationship between organisms and their environment

Educe (ih-DYUSE): v. to bring out; to deduce

Efficacy (EF-ih-kuh-see): n. effectiveness

Effectively (ih-FEK-tihv-lee): adj. actually, substantially; to all intents and purposes

Elicit (ih-LISS-uht): v. to draw forth or bring out; to derive logically

Elusive (ee-LU-sihv): adj. evading grasp or pursuit; hard to understand, define, isolate, or identify

Embargo (em-BAR-go): n. a prohibition; a legal or governmental prohibition on commerce or freight transportation

Empirical (ihm-PEER-ih-kuhl): adj. relying on or based on experiences or observation; capable of being proved by experience or observation

Engineer (in-juh-NEER): to guide the course of; to plan out, usually with some skill

Enigma (ih-NIG-muh): n. something hard to explain or understand; a mysterious or hard-to-understand person

Enterprise (IN-ter-prize): n. a hard, complicated, or risky project; a systematic activity, especially a business activity; willingness to engage in daring action

Entitlement (ihn-TITE-uhl-ment): n. the papers or other ground that support a claim

Entity (ENHT-uh-tee): n. something that exists independently or separately; the existence of a thing as contrasted with its attributes

Entrepreneur (ahn-truh-pruh-NYURE): n. one who organizes, manages, and assumes the risk of a business or enterprise

Envoy (ENN-voy, AHN-voy): n. a person delegated to represent one country in dealings with another; a messenger or representative

Epicenter (EPUH-sent-uhr): n. center; part of the earth's surface directly above an earthquake

Epiphany (ih-PIFF-uh-nee): n. an appearance, especially of a divine being; a sudden understanding of essential meaning or nature of something; an intuitive grasp of reality through something simple and striking, usually an event

Epochal (EP-uh-kuhl): adj. seasonal; uniquely or highly significant; opening a new era

Equilibrium (ee-kwi-LIB-ree-um): n. state of balance between different elements; intellectual or emotional balance

Erratic (ihr-AT-ik): adj. having no fixed course; inconsistent, irregular, or without uniformity; deviating from what is ordinary or standard

Escalate (ES-kuh-late): v. to increase in amount or intensity

Escapism (iss-KA-pizm): n. habitual diversion of the mind to entertainment or imaginative activity as an escape from reality or routine

Espouse (iss-POWZ, iss-POWSS): v. to marry; to take up and support a cause

Estuary (ESSH-chu-ware-ee): n. a water passage where the tide meets a river current, especially where the sea meets the river

Euphemism (YU-fuh-mizz-uhm): n. the substitution of an agreeable or inoffensive expression for an unpleasant or offensive one; the expression so substituted

Euphoria (yu-FOR-ee-uh): n. feeling of well-being or elation

Evasive (ih-VAY-sivv): n. tending or intended to avoid giving a direct answer

Eventuality (ih-venn-chuh-WAL-uht-ee): n. possible outcome

Evoke (ih-VOKE): v. to call forth, bring to mind; to cite, especially with approval or for support

Exact (ihg-ZAKT): v. to demand and obtain; to call for as necessary, appropriate, and desirable

Ex cathedra (ek-skuh-THAY-druh): adv., adj. (literally, from the chair) proceeding from or in the exercise of one's job or office; with authority

Excessive (ik-SESS-ihv): adj. exceeding the usual, proper, or normal

Exemplify (ig-ZEMM-pluh-fy): v. to illustrate by example; to serve as an example; to be typical of

Exonerate (ig-ZONN-uh-rate): v. to relieve from responsibility; to clear from blame

Exorbitant (ig-ZOR-buht-uhnt): adj. exceeding customary or appropriate limits

Expatriate (ek-SPAY-tree-ate): v. to leave or renounce one's country; to drive into exile, to banish

Explicit (ik-SPLISS-it): adj. fully developed; free from vagueness; externally visible

Exploit (ik-SPLOYT, EK-sployt): v. to take advantage of; to turn to economic advantage; to use unjustly or meanly for one's own advantage

Expropriate (ek-SPRPH-pree-ate): v. to deprive of possession or ownership; to transfer another's property to one's own possession

Extrapolate (ik-STRAP-uh-late): v. to protect from observed values; to predict using past experience or known data

Extraterrestrial (ek-struh-tuh-RESS-tree-uhl): adj. originating or existing outside the earth and its atmosphere

Exultant (ig-ZULT-uhnt): adj. filled with or showing great joy or triumph

Façade (fuh-SAHD): n. the front of a building, or any other of its faces given special architectural treatment; a superficial, artificial, or false appearance or effect

Faction (FAK-shun): n. a party or group within a larger group, often self-seeking or warring with the rest of the group

Falter (FALL-tuhr): v. to move or speak waveringly, hesitatingly, or weakly; to lose drive or effectiveness

Fandango (fan-DANg-go): n. a lively Spanish dance; foolish nonsense

Farcical (FAR-si-kuhl): adj. ridiculous; absurd; mocking; laughably inept

Fare (FAYR): v. to travel; to get along; to eat

Fathom (FATH-uhm): v. to take soundings; to penetrate and come to understand

Fecklessness (FECK-luhs-nuhs): n. weakness; lack of effectiveness; lack of worth or responsibility

Feign (FANE): v. to give a false impression; to pretend

Ferret (FERR-ut): v. (usually used with *out*) to find and bring to light by searching

Fervent (FUHR-vent): adj. very hot; marked by great warmth of feeling

Fete (FATE, FETT): n. festival; large elaborate party

Fiasco (fee-ASS-koh): n. a complete failure

Fiscal (FISS-kuhl): adj. relating to financial matters, especially taxation

Flamboyant (flam-BOY-uhnt): adj. ornate; given to showy display

Fledgling (FLEDJ-ling): adj. immature, inexperienced

Fluctuation (fluck-chuh-WAY-shun): n. an uncertain shifting back and forth

Fluke: n. a stroke of luck

Fob off: v. to put off with a trick or excuse; to pass off as genuine; to put aside

Foil: n. a person or thing that makes another seem better by contrast

Foment (fo-MENNT): v. to treat with moist heat; to heat up, especially in helping something grow

Foray (FOR-ay, FOH-ray): n. a sudden or irregular raid; a brief trap outside one's usual territory

Formidable (FOR-muhd-uh-buhl, for-MIDD-uh-buhl): adj. causing fear or dread; having qualities that discourage approach; tending to inspire awe

Formulation (for-myuh-LAY-shun): n. act or product of putting into a systematized statement or formula

Foster (FOSS-tuhr): to give parental care to; to promote the growth or development of

Fruitless: adj. unsuccessful

Fundamentalist (fun-duh-MENT-uh-list): n. one who believes in strictly and literally following a set of basic principles; a member of a twentieth century Protestant group that emphasizes a literal interpretation of the Bible

Furor (FYU-roar): n. an angry rage; a fashionable craze; furious or hectic activity; a public uproar

Gaffe (GAFF): n. a social error

Galvanized (GAL-vuh-nized): adj. stimulated by or as if by an electric shock; coated with zinc

Gambit (GAM-bit): n. a calculated move; a remark intended to start a conversation or make a point

Garb: n. style of dress; outward appearance

Gargantuan (gar-GANCH-uh-wuhn): adj. of tremendous size or volume

Garrulousness (GAR-uh-luhs-nuhs, GAR-yuh-luhs-nuhs): n. pointless or annoying talkativeness

Gibe (JIBE): n. taunting words; a teasing remark

Goad (GODE): n. a pointed rod used to urge on an animal; something that pricks; something that urges or stimulates into action

Grandiose (GRAN-di-ohse, gran-di-OHSE): adj. impressively large or great; characterized by affectation or grandeur or splendor; absurdly exaggerated

Grasp: n. act of seizing and holding; understanding

Gratuitous (gruh-TYU-uht-uss): adj. given unearned or without payment; costing nothing; not called for by the circumstances

Grievance (GREE-vuhnts): n. a distressing situation felt as reason for complaint or resistance; a complaint

Gross (GROSE): adj. glaringly noticeable, usually because of inexcusable badness

Ground swell: n. a broad deep ocean wave cause by a gale or earthquake; a rapid spontaneous growth

Grouse (GROWSS): v. complain, grumble

Gyrate (JY-rate): v. to revolve around an axis; to turn with (or as if with) a circular or spiral motion

Hamper: v. to interfere with; to keep from moving by way of obstacles or bonds

Hanker (HANG-ker): v. to desire strongly or persistently

Harangue (huh-RANG): v. to speak or write, especially in a noisy or pretentious manner

Harass (huh-RASS, HAR-uhs): v. to worry and impede by repeated raids; to keep annoying; to exhaust

Hawkish: adj. supporting immediate strong action, especially war or warlike policy

Heartland: n. a central and vital idea

Hinterland (HINT-uhr-land): n. an inland region; a region remote from cities or major cultural centers

Hodgepodge (HODGE-podge): n. a mixture of unrelated things

Hokum (HO-kumm): n. a device used to create a desired audience response; pretentious nonsense

Holocaust (HOLL-uh-kawst, HO-luh-kawst): n. a thorough destruction, especially by fire

Hustings (HUSS-tings): n. in some places in England and Virginia, a local court; an election platform; the proceedings or place of an election campaign

Hustle (HUSS-uhl): v. to convey or urge forward forcibly or hurriedly; to make great effort to secure money or business; to sell or get something by energetic activity, especially by fraud or deception

Hypothetical (hy-puh-THET-i-kuhl): adj. depending on supposition; not verifiable

Immediacy (im-EED-ee-uh-see): n. need to do or be done at once: act of being current, in the here and now

Imminent (IMM-uh-nent): adj. ready to take place (especially sue of a threatening possible occurrence)

Impair (im-PAIR): v. to make physically worse

Impeccable (im-PECK-uh-buhl): adj. not capable of sinning; free from fault or blame

Imperative (im-PERR-uht-iv): n. an act or duty that must be done; a command, order, rule, or guide

Implacably (im-PLAK-uh-blee): adv. unable to be made calmer, less angry, or changed in some other way

Implicit (im-PLISS-uht): adj. implied; within something's nature though not revealed, expressed, or developed; unquestioning, unhesitating

Imponderable (im-PONN-duh-ruh-buhl): adj. unable to be weighed or evaluated with exactness

Impose (im-POZE): v. to establish by force; to establish as compulsory, to force into the company or attention of someone; to take advantage

Impotent (IM-pote-uhnt): adj. lacking power, strength, or vigor; sterile

Inadvertence (in-uhd-VERT-uhnss): n. inattention; accidental oversight; the result of inattention

Incapacitate (in-kuh-PASS-uh-tate): v. to disable; to make legally incapable or ineligible

Incarnation (in-kar-NAY-shun): n. embodiment of a spirit in earthly form; time passed in a particular body or state; having a quality to a marked degree

Incendiary (in-SEN-dee-airee): adj. relating to deliberate burning of property; tending to excite or inflame

Incinerate (in-SIN-uh-rate): v. to cause to burn to cinders

Incoherent (in-co-HERE-uhnt): adj. lacking orderly arrangement; not sticking together in an orderly way

Incorrigible (in-KAWR-uh-juh-buhl): adj. not correctable; not reformable; uncontrollable

Incur (in-KUHRR): v. to bring down upon oneself, to become liable or subject to

Indigent (IN-dih-juhnt): adj. suffering poverty so sever all the comforts of life are lacking

Indiscreet (in-dis-KREET): adj. lacking good judgment in conduct or speech

Indissoluble (in-dis-OLL-yuh-buhl): adj. incapable of being dissolved or decomposed; incapable of being broken or undone, permanent

Individualist (in-duh-VIDJ-wuh-list): n. a person whose thoughts or actions are independent; a person who believes that the interests of individual people are of greatest importance

Ineffectual (in-uh-FECK-chuh-wuhl): adj. ineffective; not producing the intended effect

Ineptitude (in-EP-tuh-tyude): n. lack of competence

Inequity (in-EK-wuh-tee): n. injustice, unfairness

Inevitable (in-EV-uh-tuh-buhl): adj. unable to be avoided

Infamy (IN-fuh-mee): n. a criminal or evil act that is publicly known; a bad reputation produced by doing something shocking, brutal, or criminal

Influx (IN-flucks): n. a flowing in

Infused (in-FYUZD): adj. completely filled with or affected by something, usually for the better

Ingenuity (in-juh-NYU-uh-tee): n. cleverness in devising or designing something; a clever device or design

Ingratiating (in-GRAY-shee-ate-ing): adj. capable of winning favor; intended to win favor

Initiative (in-ISH-uh-tivv): n. an introductory step; energy or aptitude shown by beginning an action; the right to begin legislative action, or the procedure that begins legislative action

Innocuous (in-OCK-yew-uss): adj. harmless; unlikely to give offense or to arouse strong feelings, especially of hostility

Innuendo (in-yew-WEN-doh): n. a hint or insinuation, especially against character or reputation

Insatiable (in-SAY-shuh-buhl): adj. incapable of being satisfied

Insouciance (in-SOO-see-uhnss): n. lighthearted unconcern; indifference

Inspire: v. to affect, to motivate; to bring about, draw forth, or incite

Instigate (IN-stug-gate): v. to goad or urge forward

Institute (IN-stuh-tyute): v. to establish, to set going]

Insurgency (in-SURH-juhn-see): n. a condition of revolt against a government that is less than an organized revolution, and that is not recognized as a war

Integral (INT-ih-gruhl, in-TEG-ruhl): adj. formed as a unit with another part; being essential to completeness; lacking nothing essential

Interim (INT-uh-ruhm): adj. intervening, temporary

Interminably (in-TERM-uh-nuh-blee): adv. seemingly without end

Internecine (int-er-NEES-een): adj. involving conflict within a group; marked by slaughter, especially when it is mutually destructive

Interrogate (in-TERR-uh-gate): v. to question formally and systematically

Intervene (int-uhr-VEEN): v. to come between; to interfere in another nation's internal affairs

Intimidate (in-TIM-uh-date): v. to frighten; to compel with or as if with threats

Intransigence (in-TRANTS-uh-jentss): n. refusal to compromise or to abandon an extreme position or attitude

Intrusive (in-TRUE-sivv): adj. going or coming where one is not wanted or invited; projecting forward

Inured (in-YURED): adj. accustomed to accept something undesirable

Invocation (in-vuh-KA-shun): n. the act of asking for help or support; a calling upon someone for authority or justification; a legal or moral enforcement

Irrelevant (ir-RELL-uh-vuhnt): adj. beside the point

Irreverent (ir-REV-uh-ruhnt, ir-REV-ruhnt): lacking proper respect in speech or action; joking or light in manner or quality

Jape: n. something designed to amuse, especially something mocking

Jest: v. to taunt; to speak or act without seriousness; to make a witty remark

Jockey: v. to deal shrewdly or fraudulently with; to change position in a series of movements; to maneuver for advantage, especially by clever or devious means; to drive, operate

Jubilant (JU-buh-luhnt): adj. filled with or showing great joy

Junta (HUN-tuh, JUHN-tuh): n. a political or government committee, especially a group controlling a government after a revolutionary seizure of power

Jurisdiction (jauhra-uhs-DICK-shun): n. the power or right to interpret and apply the law; the authority of a power to govern; the limits within which authority may be exercised

Kamikaze (kahm-ih-KAHZ-ee): adj. relating to a Japanese World War II air unit assigned to make suicidal crashes on targets; suicidal

Klaxon (KLACK-suhn): n. an electrically operated horn or warning signal

Laconic (luh-KAHN-ick): adj. using minimum words; concise to the point of seeming rude or mysterious

Lambaste (also lambast) (LAM-baste, lam-BASTE): v. to assault violently; to attack verbally

Lamentation (lamm-uhn-TAY-shun) n. a cry of grief

Languor (LANg-goor): n. weakness or weariness of mind or body; listlessness, slowness, inertia

Latent (LAYT-nt): adj. present invisibly or inactively but able to become visible or active

Laud (LAWD): v. to praise

Lavishly (LAV-ish-lee): adj. as if poured out heavily; abundantly

Lax: adj. not firm or rigid

Laze: v. to pass the time idly or in relaxation

Legacy (LEG-uh-see): n. a willed gift, especially of money or other personal property; something received from an ancestor, a predecessor, or the past

Legitimacy (li-JIT-uh-muh-see): n. the quality of being lawful, lawfully gotten, or conforming to recognized principles or accepted rules and standards

Levy (LEVV-ee): n. the collection of money; the amount of money raised by collection

Lieu (LEW): n. place; in the lieu of; instead of

Limbo (LIMM-bow): n. place for souls barred from Heaven because unbaptized; place or state of confinement; an intermediate or transitional place or state

Liquidation (lick-wuh-DAY-shun): n. a getting rid of, killing; a settlement of a debt; a conversion of assets into cash

Litigation (lit-uh-GAY-shun): n. a legal dispute

Litigious (luh-TIDGE-uss): adj. prone to start lawsuits; of, relating to, or marked by legal dispute

Lodge: v. to settle in or occupy a place; to come to rest; to deposit for safeguard; to put before a proper authority

Logjam: a jam-up of logs in a water course; a deadlock or impasse

Ludicrous (LEWD-uh-kruhs): adj. amusing because of obvious absurdity or exaggeration; meriting scorn as being absurdly inept, false or foolish

Lumps: n. beatings; deserved penalty

Lustrous (LUHS-truss): adj. reflecting light evenly; radiant

Macabre (muh-KAHB-re, muh-KAHB-er): adj. having to do with death, especially death represented as a person; dwelling on the gruesome; tending to cause horror in the beholder

Magnific (mag-NIFF-ick): adj. magnificent; imposing in size or dignity; exalted; pompous

Malice (MAL-uhs): n. desire to see another suffer; intent to act unlawfully or cause harm without legal justification or excuse

Malign (muh-LINE): adj. evil in nature, influence, or effect; harmful; intensely and often viciously ill-willed

Malign: v. to tell misleading false reports about; to speak badly of

Mammoth (MAM-uth): adj. of great size

Manipulate (muh-NIP-yuh-late): v. to handle or manage skillfully; to control or change by unfair or tricky means, especially to serve one's own purpose

Marginal (MAHRJ-nuhl, MAHRJ-uh-nuhl): adj. located at the border; near the lower limit of acceptability or function

Martial (MAR-shuhl): adj. relating to war, a warrior, the army, or military life; warlike

Matinal (MAT-n-uhl): adj. early

Mawkish: adj. having a dull, often unpleasant taste; being sickly or childishly sentimental

Meander (me-AN-der): v. to follow a winding course; to wander casually

Mediocre (meed-ee-OH-ker): adj. ordinary; inferior in quality

Memorabilia (mem-uh-ruh-BILL-ee-uh): n. things worth remembering; records of such things

Menial (ME-nee-yuhl): adj. relating to servants; lowly, humble; lacking interest or dignity

Mentor (MEN-tore, MEN-ter): n. a trusted counselor, tutor, coach, or guide

Mercurial (muhr-KYUR-ee-uhl): adj. having rapid and unpredictable mood changes

Metaphor (MET-uh-fore, MET-uh-fer): n. a substitution of one word or phrase for another in order to express a similarity between the two ideas dealt with in the substitution

Methodology (meth-uh-DOLL-uh-gee): n. a particular procedure or set of procedures; the analysis of the principles or procedures of inquiry in a particular field

Meticulous (muh-TCIK-yuh-luss): adj. extremely or excessively careful in

Millennium (muh-LENN-ee-uhm): n. a thousand years; a thousandth anniversary; the thousand years predicted in the Bible during which Christ will reign on earth; a period of great happiness or human perfection

Mimic (MIM-ick): v. to imitate; to ridicule by imitation

Minuscule (also miniscule) (MIN-uhs-kyule): adj. very small miscalculation

Minuscule: n. mistake in figuring

Moderate (MAHD-uh-rate): v. to lessen in intensity or extremeness; to act as chairman of

Mogul (MOW-gull): n. a great person; a bump in a skid run

Momentum (mow-MENT-uhm, muh-MENT-uhm): n. the property of a moving body or action that keeps it moving unless acted on by an outside force

Monologist (also monologuist (MAHN-uhlog-sit)) (muh-NAHL-uh-just, MAHN-uh-luj-ist): n. one who gives one or more solo dramatic speeches; one who monopolizes conversation with long speeches

Moratorium (more-uh-TORE-ee-um): n. a waiting period set by an authority, especially a delay in debt payment; a suspension of activity

Mordant (MORD-nt, more-DENT); adj. biting and raustic, incisive; burning; pungent

Moribund (MORE-uh-buhnd): adj. being is a state of dying

Mortification (mort-uh-fuh-KAY-shun): n. denial of the body's needs by abstinence or discomfort; humiliation and shame caused by something that hurts the pride or self-respect; the cause of such shame

Mount: v. to increase in amount; to lift up, get up, go up; to launch and carry out

Muck: n. moist manure; slimy dirt, mud; slanderous or unflattering remarks or writing

Mufti (MUFF-tee): n. civilian clothes

Municipality (my-niss-uh-PAL-uh-tee): n. a political unit that is incorporated and usually governs itself

Muted (MYEWT-uhd): adj. toned down, quieted, silent

Myriad (MERE-ee-uhd): adj. a great many; being uncountable

Negotiate (ni-GO-shee-ate): v. to confer in order to settle a matter, especially by compromise; to deal with; to successfully travel over, complete, or accomplish; to convert into cash

Nettle: v. to sting; to arouse to sharp fleeting annoyance or anger

Noncommittal (nahn-kuh-MIT-l): adj. giving no clear indication of attitude or feeling; having no clear character

Nostrum (NAHS-trumm): n. questionable or ineffective remedy or scheme; secretly formulated medicine recommended by its preparer but usually without scientific proof of its effectiveness

Nurture (NER-cher): v. to supply with nourishment; to further the development of, to educate

Obliging (uh-BLY-jing): adj. willing to do favors; accommodating

Obliquely (oh-BLEEK-lee): adv. at an angle; not straightforwardly; indirectly; underhandedly

Obliterate (uh-BLIT-uh-rate): v. to obscure or wear away; to remove all trace; to cancel; to remove from memory; to make unrecognizable

Obsolete (ahb-suh-LETE, AHB-suh-lete): n. no longer in use; outmoded

Obstructionist (uhb-SRUCK-shun-ist): n. one who deliberately interferes with progress or business, especially that of a legislative body

Ocher (also ochre) (OH-ker): n. an earthy, red-yellow pigment made from iron ore; a muddy red-yellow color

Offensive (uh-FENT-sivv): n. an attack

Officious (uh-FISH-uhs): adj. meddlesome, offering one's services where neither needed nor wanted

Oligarch (AHL-uh-gark, OH-luh-gark): n. a member or supporter of government by a small group, especially one that controls for selfish purposes

Ominous (AHM-uh-nuss): adj. warning or foretelling, especially of something bad to come

Orgy (OR-jee): n. drunken partying; a sexually abandoned party; an action or event that shows abandon or lack of control

Ostensibly (ah-STENT-suh-blee): adv. apparently; in appearance, though not necessarily in fact

Oust: v. to remove from position, authority, or property rights, especially by force or legal action; to take the place of

Outmoded: adj. no longer stylish, usable, or acceptable

Overarching: adj. forming an overhead arch; all-embracing; dominating

Overextension (oh-vuh-rick-STEN-shun): n. commitment, especially financially, beyond a safe or reasonable point

Overt (UH-vert, OH-vert): adj. open to view

Pacifist (PASS-uh-fuhst): n. one who is opposed to war or violence as a mean of settling disputes, or who refuses to bear arms; one who refuses to resist actively

Palaver (puh-LAV-uhr, puh-LAHV-uhr): n. a long talk, usually between persons of different cultures; idle or misleading talk

Panacea (pan-uh-SEE-uh): n. a cure-all

Panglossian (pan-GLOSS-ee-uhn): adj. believing that everything happens for the best and this is the best of all possible worlds

Paradigm (PAR-uh-dime, PAR-uh-DIMM): n. an especially clear or typical example

Paradox (PAR-uh-docks): n. a statement that seems contradictory yet may be true; a self-contradictory statement that seems true at first; something or someone with seemingly contradictory qualities or phases

Parity (PAR-uh-tee): n. being equal or having the same value, especially in buying power

Parochial (puh-RO-kee-uhl): adj. relating to a church parish; confined or restricted to a parish; limited in range or scope

Parody (PAR-uh-dee): n. a close imitation for comic or ridiculing effect; a poor or silly imitation

Pedestrian (puh-DESS-tree-uhn): adj. going on foot; related to walking; commonplace, unimaginative

Peevish: adj. ill-tempered, obstinate

Penchant (PEN-chunt): n. a strong liking

Penury (PEN-yuh-ree): n. oppressive lack of resources, especially extreme poverty; extreme and often stingy care in spending money

Perceive (per-SEEVE): v. to become aware of or understand, especially through the senses

Perfunctory (per-FUNCK-tuh-ree): adj. performed routinely, mechanically, or unwillingly; lacking in interest or enthusiasm

Permeate (PER-mee-ate): v. to spread throughout

Perspective (per-SPECK-tivv): n. the way something is seen, especially with respect to relative distance and position; the ability to view things in true relation or relative importance

Pervade (per-VADE): v. to spread throughout every part

Perverse (per-VERSE): n. turned away from what is good, correct, or proper; obstinate, especially in opposing what is right or accepted; cranky; contrary to evidence

Phalanx (FAY-lanks): n. body of close-standing troops; a massed arrangement of persons, animals, or things; an organized group of persons

Pilfer (PILL-fer): v. to steal, usually stealthily and over and over, in small amounts

Plausible (PLAW-zuh-buhl): adj. seemingly worthy of belief; seeming fair or reasonable

Plethora (PLETH-uh-ruh): n. an excess

Ploy: n. a tactic, especially one designed to embarrass or frustrate an opponent; something devised or contrived

Podium (PODE-ee-um): n. a platform for an orchestra conductor; a small table on which to rest a speaker's notes; a place of formality

Poignant (POY-nyuhnt): adj. deeply or painfully affecting; pleasurably stimulating; cutting; to the point

Polarization (po-luh-ruh-ZA-shun): n. division into two opposites, especially opposite factions or groups

Polymathic (poll-ih-MATH-ic): adj. having or showing encyclopedic knowledge; very learned

Ponder (PAHN-der): v. to think about, especially quietly, soberly, and deeply; to weigh in the mind

Populist (POP-yuh-luhst): n. a believer in the right, wisdom, or virtues of the common people

Portage (POR-tihj): v. to move gear, especially overland from one body of water to another

Portend (por-TEND): v. to signify; to give an omen of

Posh: adj. elegant; fashionable

Postulate (PAHS-chuh-late): v. to demand; to claim, especially to claim as true, existent, or necessary

Potent (POTE-nt): adj. powerful, effective

Pragmatist (PRAG-muht-ist): n. one who believes in taking a practical approach to things

Prattle: n. chatter, empty talk

Precipice (PRESS-uh-puss): n. a very steep or overhanging place; the brink of disaster

Precipitate (prih-SIP-uh-tate): v. to move or make happen abruptly; to come suddenly into some condition

Preclude (pri-KLUDE): v. to prevent; to do something that makes another thing impossible

Predecessor (PRED-uh-sess-uhr): n. one who has previously occupied a place that someone else now has

Preemptive (pree-EMP-tivv): adj. taking the place of; taking for oneself; taking before others can do so; having the power to take for oneself or before others

Preoccupied (pree-AHK-yuh-PIDE): adj. lost in thought

Prerequisite (pree-RECK-wuh-zuht): adj. needed in order to carry out a function

Presage (PRESS-idge, pri-SAGE): v. to warn or predict; to have a premonition of

Primer (PRIMM-uhr): n. a small book for teaching children to read; a small introductory book on a subject

Probe: n. a tool used in surgery to examine a cavity; a device used to explore or send information from outer space; a penetrating or critical investigation; a tentative exploration

Problematic (prahb-luh-MAT-ick): n. puzzling, bewildering; unsettled; possible; open to question or debate

Profess (pruh-FESS, proh-FESS): v. to declare or admit freely; to pretend; to claim to know

Professed: adj. freely stated; pretended; claiming to be qualified

Profound (pruh-FOUND): adj. coming from, reaching to, or being down deep; showing deep feeling; full of insight; hard to understand; complete

Prohibitively (pro-HIN-uht-iv-lee): adv. tending to prevent or restrain; tending to prevent the use or acquisition of something

Proliferate (pro-LIFF-uh-rate): v. to grow or cause to grow by rapid production of new parts; to multiply

Prominent (PRAHM-uh-nent): adj. standing out beyond a surface; easily noticed; widely known

Propensity (pruh-PEN-suht-ee): adj. a strong natural inclination

Propound (pruh-POUND): v. to offer for discussion or consideration

Proscribe (pro-SCRIBE): v. to publish the name of a person condemned to death with all property forfeited to the state; to condemn or forbid as harmful; to ostracize

Protégé (PROTE-uh-zhay): n. one under the care and protection of an influential person, usually to further a career

Province (PRAHV-uhnts): n. a division of a country; a proper or appropriate function; a sphere of knowledge, influence, or activity

Provocative (pruh-VAHK-uht-ivv): n. tending to arouse, excite, or stimulate; tending to stimulate thought

Prudent (PRUDE-nt): adj. marked by wisdom or sound judgment; discreet; shrewd in managing practical affairs

Prune: v. to cut off parts for better growth; to cut away what isn't wanted

Pseudo (SUDE-oh): adj. being false or make-believe

Pseudonym (SUDE-n-im): n. false name, especially one used by a writer

Puerile (PYUR-uhl, PYUR-ile): adj. young; childish, silly

Puffery (PUFF-uh-ree): n. flattering, often exaggerated publicity

Pullulate (PUHL-yuh-late): v. to sprout; to breed or produce freely; to swarm

Punitive (PYU-nuht-ivv): adj. inflicting or aimed at punishment

Purge (PERJ): v. to free, especially from guilt; to get rid of, especially because deemed undesirable, treacherous, or unloyal

Purported (per-PORT-ed): adj. believed, rumored

Putative (PYUT-uht-ivv): adj. commonly accepted or supposed; assumed to exist or to have existed

Quantum (KWAHNT-uhm) (pl quanta): n. particle of energy; amount, part

Quantum jump, quantum leap: n. abrupt change or sudden increase

Quest (KWEST): n. pursuit, search; investigation

Quiescent (KWY-es-nt): adj. inactive; causing no trouble or symptoms

Raffish: adj. marked by or suggesting flashy vulgarity or careless unconventionality

Ramification (rem-uh-fuh-KA-shun): n. outgrowth or consequence

Rapprochement (ra-prosh-MAHNH): n. an establishment of cordial relations

Ratify (RAT-uh-fy): v. to formally approve

Rationale (rash-uh-NAL): n. an explanation for a belief, practice, opinion, or happening; an underlying reason

Raucous (RAW-kuss): adj. disagreeably harsh; noisily disorderly

Recant (re-KANT): v. to openly confess an error; to publicly withdraw a statement or belief

Reconstitute (re-KON-stuh-tyute): v. to restore to a former condition

Redress (ri-DRESS, REE-dress): v. to set right; to make up for; to remove the cause of; to avenge

Refute (ri-FYUTE): v. to disprove with argument or evidence; to deny the accuracy or truth of

Regime (ray-ZHEEM, re-JEEM): n. a way or form of government; a government in power; a period of rule

Reinstatement (ree-in-STATE-ment): n. restoration to a previous state or position

Reiterate (re-IT-uh-rate): v. to say or do again, or again and again

Relevant (RELL-uh-vuhnt): adj. having important bearing on the matter at hand, especially offering evidence that proves or disproves it

Relinquish (ri-LING-kwish): v. to leave behind; to retreat from or give up; to stop; to release; to yield

Relish (RELL-ish): v. to eat or drink with pleasure; to have a pleasing hire; to appreciate

Renascence (ri-NASS-ents, ri-NASE-nts): n. rebirth; restrengthening

Rendering (REN-durh-ing): n. a copy or version

Rendezvous (RAHN-di-voo, RAHN-day-voo): n. a meeting at a set place and time; the place of the meeting; a popular meeting place

Renown (ri-NOWN): n. fame

Renunciation (ri-nun-see-AY-shun): n. rejection; self-denial

Replete (ri-PLETE): adj. well-fed; filled

Repressive (ri-PRESS-ivv): adj. acting to put or hold down by force; preventing natural or normal expression, activity, or development

Repudiate (ri-PYUDE-ee-ate): v. to refuse to accept, acknowledge, pay, or have anything to do with; to reject as untrue or unjust

Requisition (rek-wuh-ZISH-uhn): v. to ask or demand supplies or other needs, especially in writing

Seep: v. to flow slowly through small openings

Sentient (SEN-chunt, SENT-ee-uhnt): n. aware, especially to impressions of the senses; sensitive in feeling

Seriocomic (sir-ee-oo-KAHM-ick): adj. combining the serious and the comic

Severance (SEV-uh-ruhntz): n. the act or state of being cut or ended

Shard: n. a small, usually brittle fragment

Sheaf: n. a bundle

Shore up: v. to give support to

Shortfall: n. a failure to come up to a goal or need; the amount of the failure

Shrewd: adj. clever and aware; given to cleverly tricky ways of dealing

Simplistic (sim-PLISS-tick): adj. tending to oversimplify or be oversimplified, especially by ignoring complicating factors

Simulate (SIM-yuh-late): v. to copy outwardly, often in order to deceive; to be a superficial copy

Simultaneously (sy-muhl-TAY-nee-us-lee): adv. at the same time

Skepticism (SKEP-tuh-siz-uhm): n. an attitude of doubt or suspended judgment

Skewed: adj. slanted in one direction or to one side

Sleazy (SLEE-zee): adj. carelessly or cheaply made; cheap or shoddy

Smug: adj. very self-satisfied

Solace (SAHL-us, SOLE-uhs): n. comfort, consolation; source of consolation

Sorely: adv. painfully; extremely

Souped-up: adj. increased in power or efficiency

Specter (also spectre) (SPEK-tuhr): n. a ghost; something that haunts the mind

Spectrum (SPECK-truhm): n. a continuous sequence or range

Speculate (SPECK-yuh-late): v. to think about something casually and inconclusively; to take a business risk in hope of gain

Splat: n. a splattering or slapping sound

Spoils: n. something gained by special effort; public office gained by political winners

Spontaneous (spahn-TAY-nee-uss): adj. arising from natural feeling or momentary impulse; developing without apparent external influence

Spoor (SPOOR, SPORE): n. a track or trail, especially that of a wild animal

Sporadic (spuh-RAD-ick): adj. occurring from time to time

Spree: n. an unrestrained outburst of activity, a binge

Spunky: adj. full of spirit

Spurious (SPYURE-ee-uss): adj. illegitimate; having only outward similarity; forged or of wrongly attributed origin; deceitful

Squabble (SKWAB-uhl): n. a noisy quarrel, usually over trifles

Squat: adj. low to the ground; disproportionately low or thick

Squib n. a short news item; a funny or satiric short speech or writing

Stabilize (STAY-buh-lize): v. to become, make or hold steady; to limit in fluctuation; to establish a minimum price for

Stagnation (stag-NAY-shun): n. quality of being motionless or inactive; act of becoming stagnate

Stampede (stam-PEED): n. a wild headlong rush of frightened animals; a mass movement of people on common impulse

Stigmatize (STIG-muh-tize): v. to mark or brand; to describe or identify as being shameful or contemptible

Straggle: v. to wander off course; to wander away from others of its kind

Strangulated (STRANG-gyuh-late-uhd): adj. excessively constricted, to the point of being strangled; violently destroyed.

Strife: n. fight, struggle; angry, often violent conflict; struggle for superiority

Stringent (STRIN-juhnt): adj. tightly bound; strict or severe, especially about rules or standards; marked by scarce money and restricted credit

Stump: to baffle; to walk heavily and clumsily; to travel making political speeches or supporting a cause

Suave (SWAHV): adj. smooth in performance or finish; smoothly but often superficially polite and friendly

Substantive (SUHB-stahn-tivv): adj. real rather than apparent; essential; permanent; substantial

Subversion (suhb-VUHR-zhuhn): n. overthrow, especially governmental overthrow by persons working secretly within the country

Succumb (suh-KUMM): v. to yield to greater force or to very great appeal or desire; to be brought to an end by destructive forces

Sunder (SUN-duhr): v. to break apart, especially with violence

Sway: n. a controlling influence; ruling power; the ability to influence or control

Swelter (SWELL-tuhr): v. to suffer from heat

Symposium (sim-POH-zee-um): n. a formal meeting at which several specialists give short speeches on a topic or related topics; a collection of opinions on a subject, especially if published in a journal; a discussion

Syntax (SIN-tax): n. a connected or oderly system for the arrangement of parts; the way in which words are put together to form phrases, clauses, or sentences

Tack: n. a course or method of action

Tangible (TAN-juh-buhl): adj. able to be touched; real; capable of being appraised at actual or approximate value

Tedious (TEED-ee-us): adj. tiresomely dull or long; boring telling; weighty; effective

Terminate (TUHR-muh-nate): v. to end, to form the end of, to reach an end, to serve as an end to; to discontinue the employment of

Theological (thee-oh-LODGE-ih-kuhl): adj. relating to religion or religious study

Tithe (TYTHE): n. a small tax

Titillation (titt-uhl-AY-shun): n. pleasurable excitation

Toxic (TOCK-sick): adj. poisonous; affected by a poison

Transcend (trants-SEND): v. to rise above or go beyond the limits of; to go beyond ordinary limits; to outdo in some way

Transgression (trants-GRESH-un): n. the act of going beyond set limits, especially in violation of a command, duty, or law

Transience (TRANCH-unts): n. the quality or state of being transitory, of remaining only briefly; the quality or state of affecting something or producing results beyond itself

Traumatize (TRAW-ma-tize): v. to cause injury, especially emotional injury, to someone

Trepidation (trepp-uh-DAY-shun): n. worry; apprehension

Trite: adj. commonplace; overused

Triumvirate (try-UM-vuhr-uht): n. a group of three, especially three rules

Troika (TROY-ka): n. a Russian vehicle drawn by three horses abreast; a group of three, especially closely related persons or things

Trumped-up: adj. untruthfully put together

Ubiquitous (yu-BICK-wuht-us): adj. being everywhere at the same time; constantly encountered

Ultimately (UHL-tuh-muht-lee): adv. in the end; finally

Unadulterated (un-uh-DULL-tuh-ray-tuhd): adj. pure, unmixed

Unconscionable (un-KON-shun-uh-buhl): adj. not guided by conscience, unscrupulous; unreasonable, excessive; shockingly unfair or unjust

Unduly (un-DYU-lee): adv. excessively

Unilateral (yu-nih-LAT-uh-ruhl): adj. having only one side; produced on or directed toward one side; one-sided

Unmitigated (un-MIT-uh-gate-uhd): adj. not lessened; incapable of change or of being changed

Unprecedented (un-PRESS-uh-dent-uhd): adj. never having happened before; wonderful; extraordinary

Unprepossessing (un-pree-po-ZESS-ing): adj. unattractive; uninfluential

Untempered (un-TEM-puhrd): adj. undiluted; unrestrained

Urbane (uhr-BANE): adj. very polite and smooth in manner

Urchin (UHR-chin): n. a mischievous child; a child of the streets

Utopian (yu-TOE-pee-uhn): adj. having or relating to ideal perfection, or a place of such; impossibly ideal; proposing impractically ideal schemes

Vacuity (va-KYU-uh-tee): n. empty space; state or fact of being empty, idle lacking in ideas or intelligence

Vehicle (VEE-uh-kuhl): n. a carrier or means of carrying; a medium through which something is achieved or displayed

Vendetta (ven-DETT-uh): n. a long, bitterly hostile feud

Veritable (VER-uht-uh-buhl): adj. real, authentic (often used to underscore aptness of a metaphor)

Vernal (VUHR-nuhl): adj. relating to spring; fresh, new; youthful

Viable (VY-uh-buhl): adj. able to live or grow, especially as an independent unit; able to work or develop adequately

Vicarious (vy-KARE-ee-us): adj. substituting for someone or something imaginative or sympathetic participation in someone else's experience

Vie (vy): v. to battle for superiority; to rival

Vindicate (VIN-dick-ate): v. to avenge, exonerate, justify, or defend

Vintage (VIN-tuhj): adj. of old, recognized, or lasting interest, importance or quality

Virtually (VUHRCH-uh-wuh-lee): adv. almost entirely; for all practical purposes

Visceral (VIS-uh-ruhl): adj. felt in, or as if in, the guts; instinctive; dealing with crude or elemental emotions

Volatile (VAHL-uht-l): adj. lighthearted; easily aroused; explosive; change; difficult to get or hold permanently

Vogue (VOAG): n. popularity; period of being in fashion; something in fashion at a particular time

Vulpine (VUHL-pine): adj. like a fox; tricky, sly

Waive (WAVE): v. to let go voluntarily; to keep from enforcement; to postpone from consideration

Wage: v. to engage in or carry on

Wan (WAHN): adj. sickly, pale; lacking strength; faint

Zealous (ZELL-uhss): strongly, even fanatical interested in or devoted to

Conclusion

When I thought about attempting to write this book, I asked God the main question, "What should I write about?" The answer came in quiet thoughts, silent moments, "About what you do…about what you know."

I have always felt that we are only at our best when we are giving of ourselves, the one gift no one else can give. So this is my gift, my seed – if you will – to you. I pray that you will utilize the material to its fullest, and when you have completed your task, will pass this book along to others you feel will benefit from it. This work is not about money, recognition, educational promotion, or ego; it is about sharing material that may be of benefit to others and those they come in contact with.

Thank you for your interest and your future efforts, and congratulations on your future successes. Finally, this closing note from Victor Hugo or George Eliot or possibly a Quaker missionary by the name of Grellet; no one really knows, or even if they were spoken or written:

I shall pass through this world but once.
Any good therefore that I can do, or any
Kindness that I can show to any human
Being, let me do it now. Let me not defer
Or neglect it, for I shall not pass this
Way again.

BIBLIOGRAPHY

[1] Kearsey, Cynthia. *Unstoppable*. Sourcebooks, Inc, 1998. p278-79.

[2] Waitley, Denis. *Seeds of Greatness*. Old Tappan, New Jersey: Fleming H. Revell Publishers, 1983.

[3] Postman, Neil. *The End of Education*. New York: Alfred A. Knopf Publishers, 1996. p43.

[4] Ibid., p48.

[5] Waitley, Denis. USANA Promo Tape. USANA Inc., 4550 South Main, Salt Lake City, UT, 1996.

[6] Kozol, Jonathan. *Illiterate America*. Ancho Press/Doubleday Publishers, 1985. p4.

[7] Ford, Joe Taylor. "The Executive Speechwriter Newsletter," Vol. 3, No. 2. Emerson Falls, St. Johnsbury, VT 05819.

[8] Nightegale, Earl. *This is Earl Nightengale*. New York: J.G. Ferguson Publishing, 1969. p88.

[9] Ibid., p250

[10] Nigtengale, Earl. *This Is Earl Nightengale*. New York: J.G. Ferguson Publishing, 1969. p264.

[11] Kouzes, James M. and Posner, Barry Z. *The Leadership Challenge*. Josey-Bass Publishers, 1987. p63.

[12] Meer, Jeff. *Psychology Today*, July 1986.

[13] Bronowski, Jacob. *The Ascent of Man*. Little-Brown and Company, 1973. p436.

[14] Will, George. *The Leveling Wind*. New York: Viking Publishing, 1994. p199.

[15] Nightengale, Earl. *This Is Earl Nightengale*. New York: J.G. Ferguson Publishing, 1969. p88.

[16] Postman, Neil. *Conscientious Objections*. New York: Alfred A. Knopf, Inc., 1988. p173.

[17] Dyer, Wayne W. *Your Sacred Self*. New York: Harper Collins Publishers, 1995. p103.

[18] Postman, Neil. *The End of Education*. New York: Alfred A. Knopf Publisher, 1996. p103.

[19] Bennett, William J. *The Devaluing of America*. New York: Summit Books, 1992. p226.

[20] Ibid., p226-27.

[21] Ford, Joe Taylor. "The Executive Speechwriter Newsletter." Vol. 1, No. 2, Emerson Falls, St. Johnsbury, VT 05819.

[22] Johnson, Raymond Coles. *The Achievers*. New York: E.P. Dutton Publishers, 1987.

[23] Ragan Communications, Inc. Speaker's Idea File, 212 West Superior Street, Chicago, IL 60610.

[24] "A return to Love" by Marianne Williamson (as quoted by Nelson Mandela in his inaugural speech, 1994). *The Power of Focus* by Jack Canfield, Health Communications, Inc., Publishers, Deerfiedl Beach Florida, 2000. pp158-159.

[25] Excerpt from "Ambition: The Secret Passion" by Joseph Epstein.

[26] Quotation from "The Himalayan Expedition," by W.H. Murray, J.M. Dent, & Dons Publishers, Ltd., 1951.

[27] Lee, Richard G. *There's Hope For the Future*. Nashville, TN: Broadmand and Holman Publishers, 1996. p58.

[28] The Lincoln Library. New York: The Frontier Press, Thirteenth Ed., 1967. p1801.

[29] Nightengale, Earl. *Lead the Field*. Biles, Illinois: Nightengale-Conant Publishers, 1996. p55.

[30] Miller, Phyllis A. *Managing Your Reading*. Reading Development Resources, 1987.

[31] Excerpt from *Life is Not a Game of Perfect*, by Dr. Bob Rotella with Bob Cullen, Simon & Schuster, New York, 1999. pp-118,119.

[32] Jones, Judy and William Wilson. "100 Things Every College Graduate Should Know." *Esquire Magazine*, pp91-96.

[33] Tony Alessandra, Ph.D, *Charisma*. Warner Books, 1998. p 41.

[34] Harvey, Mackay. Tulsa World. October 31, 1999.

[35] Bell, James S. and Stan Campbell. *A Return to Virtue*, Northfield Publishing, 1995. p15.

[36] Golden, Frederic. "Who Got There First?" Brittanica.com 17 May 1999.

[37] *Time Magazine*. January 2,1956.

[38] Bell, James S. and Stan Campbell. *A Return to Virtue*. Northfield Publishing, 1995. p14.

[39] Gray, Alice. *Stories for the Heart*. Multnomah Publishers, Inc. 1996. p103.

[40] Gray, Alice. *Stories for the Heart*. Multnomah Publishers, Inc. 1996. p114.

[41] Maxwell, John C. *Developing the Leader within You*. Nashville: Thomas Nelson Publishers, 1993. p98-99.

[42] Success Motivation Institute, Inc. Copyright 1969.

Dr. Johnny Mac Allen is an Associate Professor of Public Relations/ Advertising in the Communication Arts Department at Oral Roberts University in Tulsa, Oklahoma.

Before becoming a professor, Allen worked in the radio and television industry for over 20 years serving in various capacities from on-air staff to management. He began his higher education career in administration where he directed public relations/advertising and communication efforts, before becoming a full-time professor. He has received numerous awards for his innovative public relations/advertising campaigns in local and national competitions. In addition, Allen received the "Outstanding Faculty Member" award for 1995-1996 from the ORU College of Arts & Sciences, and his student evaluations continue to rank him in the upper two-percent each year.

Professor Allen continues to conduct seminars and workshops for companies and ministries on marketing, advertising, and personal development. He has given numerous academic presentations in addition to publishing a wide range of articles.

He holds a bachelor's degree from the University of Central Oklahoma, a master's from the University of Oklahoma, and a doctorate from Oklahoma State University.